MELTDOWN

The Ichthyologist's Guide to the Subprime Meltdown

By Jeremy Bagott

First Edition

Band of Investment Publishing Co.
Ventura, California

ISBN: 9780-999710784

10 9 8 7 6 5 4 3 2 1

BAND OF INVESTMENT PUBLISHING CO.
2674 East Main Street, Suite E-504
Ventura, California, 93003

Disclaimer: This publication is sold with the understanding that
neither the publisher nor the author is engaged in rendering legal,
accounting or investment counseling or any other type of
professional service. If expert assistance is required, the services of
a competent professional should be sought.

Also by Jeremy Bagott

Dispatches from the Cosmic Cobra Breeding Farm

Guaconomics: Dipping a Chip into America's Besieged Party Bowl

ACKNOWLEDGMENTS

The author praises Andrew Gowers, Lehman Brothers' onetime head of communications, for his eyewitness accounts of life at the doomed investment bank; author Kate Kelly for putting quill to paper about the last days of Bear Stearns in "Street Fighters"; Barry Ritholtz, eminent diarist of the nanny state in "Bailout Nation"; Lawrence G. McDonald and Vicky Ward, authors of "A Colossal Failure of Common Sense" and "The Devil's Casino" respectively; Andrew Ross Sorkin, for his magnum opus "Too Big to Fail"; Roger Lowenstein for his 2010 book "The End of Wall Street"; and authors Michael M. Thomas and Alexandra Lebenthal for their fictional œuvres "Fixers" and "The Recessionistas" respectively. The author also hails Michael Lewis for his romp through the landscape of fiendishly impenetrable financial products and naked greed in "The Big Short." Finally, the author genuflects to writer Michael Shnayerson for his "Profiles in Panic."

The opening chapter would not be the same without the reflections of then-greenhorn Lehman analyst Alex Sienaert.

The author is grateful for the weak-but-still-beating heart of enterprise journalism. He thanks The Wall Street Journal, The Associated Press, Reuters, CBS, CNN Money, Business Insider, The Guardian, The New York Post, The Financial Times, ProPublica, Vanity Fair, The New York Times, Salon and other media outlets.

This book is dedicated to capitalism. The 2007-2008 crisis was about the erosion of consequences. Its cost was collectivized. It should horrify every believer in free markets. This book is also dedicated to the memory of the author's dear pal Dale and the sacrifice of the male anglerfish.

Contents

'Repo 105'

The "Repo 105" was like heroin.

The U.S. Securities and Exchange Commission didn't understand the Repo 105. It didn't understand a lot of things – but it certainly didn't understand the Repo 105.

"It sounded like rat poison … the Repo 105 … when I first heard it," said Matthew Lee in a very cool, upper-class British accent. Lee, in his mid-50s, was the patrician senior accountant at Lehman Brothers responsible for the investment bank's global balance sheet. If you were casting a film and needed a square-jawed Oxford don type, Lee was your pick.

Lehman used the Repo 105, an accounting maneuver, to move more than $50 billion in securities to and from its balance sheet to create the appearance it held more cash to offset some of its enormous debt.

The money was hidden behind one thousand veils. It was

a shell game.

At the end of Lehman's fiscal year, Lee refused to sign off on the accuracy of the firm's accounting practices. Then he sent a letter to Lehman's finance chief, Erin Callan. He drew her a map. But it was like pulling the pin on a hand grenade. Six days later, he was pulled out of a meeting and fired on the spot – after 14 years at the investment bank. Lehman contended Lee was downsized as part of broader work-force cuts. He says otherwise.

After he was bounced from his post, Lee, who became a key but largely unsung player in Lehman's epic implosion, took up the life of a nomad; he was seen riding a motorcycle across Australia's Outback and other remote places. He became an enigma.

But back to the Repo 105 … it was a powerful piece of accounting wizardry anyway.

Wharton finance professor Franklin Allen suggests that other firms participating in Lehman's Repo 105 transactions – namely, its auditors and law firms – must have also known the thing was a smokescreen.

Where was the Securities and Exchange Commission? The SEC was in the building – literally. It actually had regulators embedded in Lehman's glinting glass-and-steel ziggurat on Seventh Avenue in Midtown Manhattan.

"Regulators at the SEC – usually lawyers with no finance experience – are trained to look at a complex trade and pick out the misdemeanors, while they completely miss the felony," said one insider.

The modern-day regulator comes in after the fact, in this case, after the largest bankruptcy in U.S. history happens under its nose. It performs the mop-up operations, toe-tags and body-bags the victims and notifies the next of kin.

Lehman didn't have a big enough capital cushion. It was

as simple as that. It received a waiver to the Net Capitalization Rule, which required a debt-to-equity ratio no greater than 12 to 1. It kept something like a 40-to-1 ratio and shoveled mountains of borrowed cash into every shaky mortgage-backed derivative it could make or find.

The SEC talent pool just wasn't deep enough to provide the kind of mental acuity required to monitor the $1 trillion in notional value of the derivatives Lehman had alchemized. The SEC attorneys didn't have the mental wattage to keep up with the Harvard and Wharton grads who devised the ever-more complex derivatives. And with the Repo 105, Lehman could make billions disappear and reappear.

So government regulators had only what lawyers called "a road map for further inquiry" into former Lehman executives and its auditing firm, Ernst & Young.

These were interesting times, times that would culminate in Lehman's calamitous last weekend, September 13 and 14, 2008.

The mortal blow would make it the largest bankruptcy in history; its assets topped, by far, those of previously plundered behemoths like Enron and WorldCom. It would hold its ranking even after General Motors filed for Chapter 11 and Washington Mutual later fell. Yet with $639 billion in assets and $619 billion in debt, it was only the nation's fourth-largest investment bank at the time.

Lehman's brooding, iron-fisted chief executive, Richard "Dick" Fuld, Jr., was hunkered in what had become a gilded *Führerbunker* on the 31st Floor. The floor was known intramurally as "Club 31." That's what the rabble toiling on the coalface and in the building's sculleries and catacombs called it.

Fuld was not imposing in size – he stood 5-foot, 10-inches tall. It was more the severity of his gaze. The man has

Doberman pinscher eyes: intense, deep-set with dark – almost black – irises buried beneath a boney, perennially furrowed brow. The high forehead, the aquiline nose, the prognathous jaw pointed slightly skyward – all projected an air of intensity. The veins in his neck could become blood-engorged and pop out. You didn't want to be there when *that* happened.

"Those closest to him slaved like courtiers to a medieval monarch, second-guessing his moods and predilections, fretting over minute details of his schedule down to the flower arrangements." wrote Andrew Gowers, former editor of the Financial Times, who was working at Lehman when it went kablooey. "To say he was surrounded with a cult of personality would be an understatement."

Fuld, 62 at the time, retained a lean, sinewy form. A fitness buff, he was always in top shape. He was built like a Honduran welterweight prizefighter. Senior executives would sometimes order him a mid-morning plate of ribs. His ferocity alone seemed to burn through the calories. That he never gained weight could only have been seen as a triumph of mind over matter.

A New York Times profile in October 2007 painted Lehman Brothers and Fuld's persona as inextricably linked. Some senior executives at Lehman said there was a reluctance to challenge the strong-willed chief. That might have slightly understated it.

But in actual fact, very few ever saw Dick Fuld in the flesh, observed one former Lehmanite. For those who did, he had but one personality. Seen through Goffman's dramaturgical explanation of social interactions, whether Fuld was center-stage or up in the control booth, he was the same to everyone. And his demeanor was not exactly what anyone would call a barrel of laughs.

He seemed to value loyalty above all else, which was a

fatal flaw. Over time, "he was shut off from independent sources of information, from challenging questions and from up-to-date views from the front line of Lehman's daily battle in the markets," wrote Gowers. "He was fed instead with the carefully filtered facts that his inner circle thought he wanted to hear." It created a repressive regime that allowed him to exist in one reality and 26,000 necessary but inconvenient vassals in another.

Before the denizens of the 31st Floor would arrive at the building, someone would place a call to the building's security desk. A security officer would summon a nonpublic express elevator car to the building's concourse. The car was preprogrammed to go straight to the 31st Floor.

Club 31 was once the white-hot core of all power-brokering, deal-making and dynastic intrigues at the House of Lehman. But the 31st floor, by many accounts, became a quiet place – a monastery – by midafternoon. As the bank was in its death rattle, Fuld was surrounded there by his loyalists. Lehman's pixie dust was degrading by the hour.

Before the bank's final curtain, Fuld may have tried to soften his image. "He's made it more comfortable for people to speak," said Joe Gregory, Lehman's chief operating officer and Fuld's No. 2.

Of Fuld's ministers, Gregory was the most loyal. Also, he was a great fixer. Unlike Fuld, who was a one-man nor'easter, Gregory had a touchy-feely side. He was no doubt able to jolly up and wheedle the great caudillo like no one else.

But publicly, Fuld brooked little dissent, and Gregory, by all accounts, became not only Fuld's liegeman but his hatchet man. If you got crossways with Fuld, your chances of being lined up against a wall by Gregory were high.

"If Dick was the king, Joe was Cardinal Richelieu," wrote Gowers. "His job was not to encourage debate or intellectual curiosity in subordinates but to bend the bank to Dick Fuld's will."

Fuld had been Gregory's mentor going back to the 1960s, before Lehman had been snapped up by American Express, becoming "Shearson Lehman" in 1984, then "Shearson Lehman Hutton" in 1988, and then spun off by American Express to return to "Lehman Brothers" in 1994.

Over the span of three decades, Fuld and Gregory had rarely sat more than a hundred feet from one another.

"He feels betrayed," a friend of Fuld's told the New York Observer after the fall. At night, Fuld was reported to have had trouble sleeping. Even the sandman was shunning him. Most of the time, he was in Greenwich, Connecticut, in one of his five houses. He would wander the 20 rooms, the pool house, the tennis court, the squash court. Mostly, he sat and replayed Lehman's calamitous finale, ransacking his brain. "What could I have done differently? What should I have said?" It must have been surreal for Fuld – as if he had left his own body through astral projection. When Morpheus did come, it could only have been a great relief. Maybe God would come quietly in the night and whisk him away, sparing him the ignominy of this....

For an investment bank that would become totemic of American financial might, its beginnings were unremarkable. Henry Lehman, 23, son of a cattle merchant, emigrated to the United States from Bavaria in 1844. He settled in the antebellum South, opening a dry-goods store in Montgomery, Alabama, under the shingle "H. Lehman." By 1850, his two brothers had followed him to America and the firm changed its name to "Lehman Brothers."

Henry Lehman was struck dead at 33 from yellow fever while in New Orleans. His brothers, Emanuel and Mayer, stumbled into commodities trading. The business often accepted raw cotton from customers as payment for goods. Over time, trading in cotton became the most significant part of its operations.

After the Civil War, the cotton trade shifted its orbit from the South to New York City. Lehman opened a branch office at 119 Liberty Street in Lower Manhattan, and 32-year-old Emanuel moved there to run it. The firm, soon headquartered in New York, helped found the New York Cotton Exchange in 1870; Emanuel sat on its board of governors until 1884.

Lehman dealt in the emerging market for railroad bonds – the dot-com bubble of its day – and became a member of the Coffee Exchange as early as 1883 and finally the New York Stock Exchange in 1887, underwriting its first public offering in 1899 for the preferred and common stock of the International Steam Pump Company.

In 1906, it took the General Cigar Company public, followed closely by Sears, Roebuck and Company. Big things were happening in America and the up-and-coming Lehman was part of it all.

In the wake of the collapse a century later, the New York Times was reporting Fuld had sold his seaside mansion on Jupiter Island in Florida, bought for more than $13 million five years earlier, for a sawbuck to his wife. His motivation was unclear, but Fuld was under intense scrutiny from investigators after Lehman declared bankruptcy.

Once the Chapter 11 papers were filed – it took but six hours to fill out the requisite paperwork for the nation's largest bankruptcy – communications broke down between the executive suites in New York and the London offices in Canary Wharf.

One U.K. trader in Lehman's fixed-income group, a man in his mid-30s, was instructed to keep coming to work if he wished to be paid. So, he and his colleagues came in and played Pac-Man and Tetris every day until one morning, a man from PricewaterhouseCoopers called the whole London-based fixed-income group together in an auditorium and told them they were all fired. Before this mass-defenestration, the man – he who played Pac-Man and Tetris – had already watched $1 million of his Lehman stock evaporate.

By all accounts, Fuld and his wife, Kathleen – a regal blonde and former Lehman trader whom everyone called "Kathy" – had a stable, even blissful, marriage. The union was held up as a sort of consecration of Lehman ideals – a model for other executive couples. But for the wives of the firm's top executives, being part of the Lehman family meant a life of guarded behavior, loneliness and intense competition, wrote Vicky Ward, author of "The Devil's Casino."

The wives of Lehman's senior management were expected to attend fashionable charity events at places like Manhattan's Museum of Modern Art, which everyone – *tout le monde* – knew simply as "MoMA." They "were told exactly how much they had to donate," one Lehman wife told Ward.

Fuld was known to keep a keen eye on his executives' marriages, especially at the company's Sun Valley, Idaho, retreats as the Denalis and Escalades whisked Lehman couples from Friedman Memorial Airport at the base of the Sawtooth Range. No Lehmanite would dare aver an invitation to the epic retreats.

Fuld believed if the couples had stable home lives, they would be more productive at work.

A decade after the fall, some members of the Lehman diaspora described their time at the investment bank as being "part of a family." Even when the bank was in its death rattle on the Friday before it passed away.

"It was a little like you feel when you have a family

member in the hospital," Beth Anisman, Lehman's onetime global chief administrative officer for legal, compliance and audit, told the Wall Street Journal a decade later with not a hint of irony. Said Larry Bortstein, Lehman's onetime head of global technology law, with a far-off look in his eye: "I loved working there … when I think just how kind everyone was to each other. …"

But in the end, money was what it really came down to. The picnic was over.

Lehman's professorial chief legal officer, Tom Russo, described his feeling that a deus ex machina event would play out: "In the early part of the day, I thought there was going to be a deal with Barclays, and we would be saved."

Mohammed Grimeh, Lehman's global head of emerging markets, fixed income, came to the building the Sunday night of bankruptcy weekend wearing a Team France polo shirt with the No. 3 on the sleeve. It wasn't a polo-*style* shirt, but it seemed to be an actual *polo* shirt – as if the handsome thirtysomething had just been playing polo.

He told a roiling scrum of reporters outside the building that on the trading floor, which would ordinarily have been empty on a Sunday night, "people were drinking beer, [and] smoking inside." It was Lord of the Flies in there – a vice den.

Lehmanites were busy posting images of Dick Fuld and Joe Gregory with – Oh dear! Oh dear! Oh dear! – defamatory captions. The traders had turned on the denizens of Club 31 decisively. The soldiery was in open revolt.

In the sickly glimmer of the trading floor's Bloomberg terminals, morose groups huddled in ad hoc therapy sessions – sad murmurs were punctuated only by the defiant shouts of a few yahoos. In the bilious glow of the terminals a woman was crying hot tears onto the shoulder of a male co-worker.

Outside the building, in a move that became only slightly

less iconic than the flag raising on Mount Suribachi, before a vast profusion of press photographers and television cameramen, Grimeh, with a rakish air, hoisted a Lehman Brothers sign over his head. Then, seemingly magnetized by the cameras, he flashed a peace sign to the mob. It was Churchillian. The hive registered its approval with a squall of yowls and shutter clicks. It was a feasting zone for the press. Time stood still in the City of New York in the County of New York in the State of New York.

Some Lehmanites were content to melt into their sofas or vintage Eames Model 670 lounge chairs and view the whole nightmare through the bottom of a Corvina bottle. Others were drawn like excited photons to the mothership's gravitational collapse.

There had been some half-hearted attempts to right the ship, attempts that might have bought Lehman time and good will. Months before, there had been a Greek chorus of warnings. At some point in 2008, Hugh "Skip" McGee, who headed Lehman's investment banking operations, was said to have approached Fuld seeking Gregory's ouster. He believed Gregory, who was in his mid-50s at the time, was the root of many of the investment bank's ills. But by then, even sacking Gregory would be thin gruel to Wall Street.

Gregory's reputation was less for his acumen as a chief operating officer and more for his opulence. The 19th century American-Norwegian economist Thorstein Veblen coined the terms "conspicuous waste" along with "pecuniary emulation" (striving to meet or exceed someone else's financial status). Gregory seemed to be the very embodiment of these.

He had numerous homes: a 15,000 square-foot main house with a 6,000 square-foot guest home on 10 acres in Lloyd Harbor on Long Island's North Shore, where neighbors included actor Brad Pitt, Christie Brinkley and Billy Joel and the ineffable Dee Snider, singer and songwriter for the heavy metal band Twisted Sister.

Gregory also had an eight-bedroom, 9,500-square-foot oceanfront home in Bridgehampton, where neighbors included Beyoncé and hubby Jay-Z, Goldman Sachs chief Lloyd Blankfein and Madonna; a ski home in Manchester, Vermont; a $4.4 million Manhattan apartment at the Mayfair on Park Avenue; and, reportedly, a comparatively pedestrian house in the Keystone State.

"He had a kid who went to a small school in Pennsylvania," a former colleague told Michael Shnayerson of Vanity Fair magazine in 2009. "Joe didn't like the hotel, so he bought [a] house in town. It was probably only $500,000, but he paid for it so that, on the maybe two trips a year he took there, he'd have a nice place to stay. And then he had it redecorated!"

Gregory's first marriage ended in divorce in 1999. His first wife, Teresa, was described by Ward as "athletic and fun," but as not having "fit in at Lehman dinners."

After purchasing the Bridgehampton pad for $19 million in 2007, Gregory and his philanthropic-minded second wife, Niki, spent an additional couple of million renovating the new place, which sat on 2.5 oceanfront acres. Niki was a Greek-born, chestnut-haired knockout who had recently divorced when the two married in 2000. Their sons had been best friends at school.

Chez Gregory at Bridgehampton was sublime, with its two-story vestibule; its custom raised-panel joinery; its coffered ceilings; its two dining rooms; its four fireplaces; its mullioned windows; its steeply front-gabled but low-hipped roofline; its towering, almost comically magnificent chimneys.

It was 2007 – a great time to be Joe Gregory and a great time to be a purveyor of creamy porcelain table lamps with ovoid shapes and those delicate, craze-patterned cracks in the glazing; teapoys; fauteuils; curio cabinets; Sheraton armchairs; custom woven rugs; and fashionable bibelots.

Somewhere, a man might be seen in Dior pajamas and Santorini leather fisherman sandals from the Saks Fifth Avenue men's shop. The man would be speaking a couple decibels too loudly on his cell phone in the media room … or the conservatory … or the second-floor entertainment room opened to the ocean view deck … or from one of the twin master suites … or from one of the six additional bedrooms, each with an en-suite bathroom … the voice bouncing off the 10-foot ceilings on the main floor or the quarter-sawn oak plank flooring, but muffled slightly by the floral chintz draperies.

The man is instructing an underling to buy a full table at a benefit dinner along with tickets for the pre-party at the Guggenheim Foundation gala at Pier 40. The man might be looking out upon the gunite pool and spa and the private path across the dunes leading to 200 feet of swell semi-private Bridgehampton beachfront.

But, alas, it is an apparition. Joe and Niki Gregory appear to have been virtually AWOL from the Bridgehampton house since completing its renovation. They stayed at the home maybe 14 days since buying it, it was reported.

After Lehman went to its reward, Gregory tried selling the place for $32.5 million, then slashed the asking price to $27.9 million. Even with the price drop, it didn't sell and was pulled off the market. In November 2010, it went back on the market for $25 million. The following year, advertising mogul Donny Deutsch snapped it up for a relative steal – $20.5 million.

When Gregory's 90-minute commute from his Lloyd Harbor Xanadu to his Midtown Manhattan office began to weigh down on him, he bought a helicopter and a seaplane to shorten the trip. "He loved the ease of it," wrote Andrew Ross Sorkin in "Too Big to Fail." His pilot would land at the West Side Heliport, then a driver would shuttle him to Lehman Brothers' towering offices in Times Square. Door to door in under twenty minutes."

The couple was a portrait of excess during the late Lehman epoch. Author Ward reports that Niki, who had a taste for expensive shoes, gave Lehman wives tours of her enormous closets at the Lloyd Harbor home. Her shoe closets were said to be twice the size of the Jimmy Choo store on 5th Avenue. She had a personal staff of as many as 30 trusty retainers who were ready to react to her every wish without delay.

She was well-known at the Americana Manhasset mall, an upscale, open-air shopping center nicknamed the "Miracle Mile of Manhasset" on the North Shore of Long Island. Her cross-country shopping excursions were legion.

In a simpler epoch, in the teens and 1920s, after Lehman's initial public offering of Sears, many a nationally known private company entered the investment bank's maw and emerged as a publicly traded one. Lehman became a Sargasso Sea of initial public offerings, underwriting scores of new issues, often in conjunction with Goldman Sachs. Among them were what had become – or would become – revered names on the American landscape: F.W. Woolworth, May Department Stores, Gimbel Brothers, R.H. Macy & Company and industrial titans like The Studebaker Corporation, the B.F. Goodrich Company and Endicott Johnson Corporation.

Philip Lehman, Emanual's son, became a partner in the firm in 1887 and retired in 1925 as managing partner and its first chairman. He became a patron of the arts and willed much of his art collection to his son Robert "Bobbie"

Lehman, who took over as head of the firm when Philip retired. During Bobbie's reign, the company survived the Great Depression by focusing on venture capital as the equities market slowly recovered.

Now, in the smoldering carnage of early 2009, for-sale signs defiled the serene high-hedged roads across the exclusive townships that make up the Hamptons – summer playground of New York's glitterati and masters of the universe. Where secluded multimillion-dollar estates south of Route 27 once sold before they were even put on the market, data showed that in Suffolk County, there were 154 new foreclosures in July 2009, up 105 percent over the previous year. The Hamptons' reliance on Wall Street for purchases and summer rentals was becoming all too evident. The Hamptons were in crisis.

"In the 20 years I've been doing this, this is the weakest rental market I've seen," Jan Robinson, founder of boutique brokerage Hampton Homes, told a reporter. Robinson said her East Hampton rental business was down by 70 percent from 2008.

Sniffing blood in the water, prospective tenants no longer jockeyed to line up a plum rental by Presidents' Day. They were now launching their searches later – and for what earthly reason wouldn't they? – figuring rents would fall as the summer neared. They weren't wrong. Clients once forced to lease a house from Memorial Day to Labor Day were now able to negotiate a la carte rentals a month at a time, or in an unthinkable state of affairs in the Hamptons, a week at a time!

One Bridgehampton real estate broker recounted to a reporter in early 2009 that she was often the only person in her storefront office. Some brokers were rumored – horror of horrors! – to have taken retail jobs in East Hampton's Main Street stores in order to make ends meet.

One did have the feeling all along that the Hamptons would survive whatever downturn the market could throw at it and still attract the requisite roster of rappers, heirs to dry-goods fortunes, A-list actors, fashion designers, infomercial magnates and others who have the wherewithal to spend $6,500 a night on rent for an entire summer.

As president and chief operating officer beginning in 2004, Gregory came to oversee all departments, including the increasingly complicated derivatives the bank was underwriting.

The commercial paper Gregory had traded in his early days at Lehman was lower-risk. "Commercial paper" describes short-term IOUs issued by private companies. "If you bought it wrong, you could hold the position," one ex-colleague told Shnayerson, "so it would cost you a few basis points, that's all."

The longer end of the market involved bonds you might get stuck with if conditions changed. "I don't know if Gregory knew how much risk he was taking," the ex-colleague told Shnayerson. "The other thing, which Joe had never seen, was how a market could go highly illiquid. Joe had observed this but not lived it."

Gregory received $19 million in stock awards, accounting for 73 percent of his total pay in 2007. He also got $4.6 million in a non-equity incentive plan, $1.9 million in option awards and a salary of a modest $450,000 and $40,500 in other compensation. His total haul was reported to be $26 million.

Lehman employees held – and borrowed against – their stock awards. Five-year lockups kept them from liquidating some of the shares. However, it wasn't unusual for employees to hold onto their Lehman shares much longer than the five years, especially given their meteoric price growth. Lehman went from less than $10 a share in early 1996 to $78 at the close of 2006. Its market capitalization went from less than $3 billion in 1994 to $45.5 billion in early 2007.

Fuld held the largest pile of shares by a large margin. At one point, he was reported to have owned stock worth almost $1 billion – and this was apart from his stock options. Gregory had the second-largest pile. He was thought to have had $574 million in paper wealth at one point.

Lehmanites tended to borrow against their stock holdings. It turned out to be calamitous for many. The risk must have seemed minimal between 2000 and 2006, when the stock was doing nothing but appreciating. The shares must have seemed as unimpeachable as Krugerrands or Treasury notes. But if you were making $4 million a year in stock awards and salary – with most of the shares locked up for five years – you couldn't rightly be seen living the life of a pauper making a pitiable $1 million a year.

But say you wanted to be prudent – *really* prudent – and not borrow against your stock awards, relying instead on your salary alone, which you calculated would allow you to spend $2.5 million for a home. But what the hell could you even buy for $2.5 million?

Maybe … maybe … you could get a 2-bedroom renovated prewar condo on the Upper West Side in an unremarkable building that looked like one of those European train station hotels where guests stayed to take the cure. The façade might have a few Venetian Gothic grace notes – archivolts, fluted pilasters, a couple of shabby medallions with horn-blowing cherubs in low relief and maybe … maybe … hand-cut mosaic tiles and coffered ceilings in the lobby.

But now you're visiting a colleague who is lord of a prewar five-bedroom, four-and-a-half-bath co-op on the entire 17th Floor with a private elevator that opens into a private vestibule, a living room with river and city views, a Louis XVI marble fireplace with side columns and Corinthian capitals, a formal dining room, 12-foot barrel-vaulted ceilings, a private terrace and arched brick doorways with a doorman.

Now you're going to start looking at those locked-up shares as a means to an end. By all that is holy, how could providence deny you such a place? The digs you warrant? Veblen's Theory of Pecuniary Emulation even predicts it!

Based on his interviews, Shnayerson came away feeling that a Lehman banker by, say, 60, had likely salted away enough to preserve his gentility during his autumn years on a meager couple of million a year. The 25-year-olds who worked at the bank and were let go when it collapsed never earned enough to lose much. But Shnayerson believed that a legion of Lehman bankers in their mid-30s to mid-40s who had attempted to live up to their high paper compensation, and sometimes beyond it, careened toward personal ruin when Lehman imploded.

Gregory was jettisoned in June 2008. But for Lehman's survival, it was already too late. The horse was out of the barn.

Before his ouster, Gregory had reportedly played a key role in pushing out Mike Gelband, a Lehman Brothers managing director and the firm's head of global fixed income, after Gelband had given a presentation about the proliferation of "no-doc" mortgages – what came to be called "liar loans" and "ninja loans" – negative-amortization loans, no-down-payment loans, optional adjustable-rate mortgages and other radioactive products being peddled by commissioned salesmen and snapped up by Lehman.

Lawrence G. McDonald, a former Lehman vice president and author of the 2009 book "A Colossal Failure of Common Sense," recounts Gelband's presentation:

"He cited the shadow banks, the vast complex network

of mortgage brokers that were not really banks at all but managed somehow to insert themselves into the lending process, making an enormous number of mortgages possible."

In his presentation, writes McDonald, Gelband pointed to companies like Countrywide, New Century, HBOS and NovaStar, accusing them of creating over $1 trillion in false, empty economic activity that simply transferred risk to Wall Street. He described the now-routine practice by homeowners of using their residences as ATMs, pulling out cash each time their home values increased.

Those who learned of Gelband's briefing were described as looking "somewhat bewildered." At least a few young bucks with shaped cuticles and bench-made full-brogue Oxfords suspected Gelband of being some querulous curmudgeon or attention-seeking apostate or contrarian sitting on a pile of credit-default swaps … or … quite possibly … deranged. At the least … the very least … this was someone hopelessly weighed down by a single-variable mindset (but complete derangement was not off the table).

This deeply puzzling figure portrayed economists as being out of touch and unable to understand the stimulus effect the derivatives were now having on the economy. Gelband even used his position on the investment bank's executive committee to urge Lehman to switch horses, to reduce its exposure to the toxic asset-backed paper.

But Gelband's *cris de coeur* fell on deaf ears. After having lunch with Gregory, he resigned. It had been a hanging offense. Like the medieval heretic John Wycliff, he was burned alongside his writings – or in this case, his PowerPoint.

Then, in turn, Fuld reluctantly offered up Gregory's head to please the Street and buy precious time. Immediately after the latter's sacking, the idea bubbled up in Gregory's mind to ask Lehman for a loan against his stock, which was still locked up, according to New York magazine. Certainly, he would be able to get at the money in one form or another. He probably had that outcome comfortably in mind.

But then Lehman became a caustic cloud of gamma-ray-emitting antimatter. In retrospect, even if all his shares had been available, he would have had only a very narrow window to sell them before Lehman fell in on itself with the pressure of 10,000 Earth atmospheres. Events conspired to scotch any hope of this. Speculation is rife that Gregory's paper wealth simply disintegrated when the doomed investment bank met its fiery death. Gregory must have been hemorrhaging money at that point.

To raise cash, he put his properties up for sale. The Park Avenue apartment found a buyer in October for $4.4 million. He sold his helicopter and by and by, his Bridgehampton and Lloyd Harbor homes. In 2009, he filed a $233 million claim against Lehman's estate to recover deferred stock compensation. Gregory wanted the investment bank to make him whole for money he believed he earned while helping to wreck the place.

Gregory, who had worked with Fuld for almost four decades, focused a significant amount of his time on Lehman's "culture."

Gregory "seemed to regard the firm's finances as a distraction from sundry other subjects, such as employee diversity or his newly built $32 million oceanfront home in the Hamptons," wrote Roger Lowenstein in his 2010 book "The End of Wall Street."

One observer labeled him "diversity-obsessed," to the detriment of managing the firms' core activities and managing its risk. So he dabbled, *noblesse oblige*, on the firm's culture. "We believe we have something unique," he rhapsodized to a reporter. "I worry about how to keep it, or keep what is good about it."

In the months and years after Lehman's demise, the transitory nature of "ownership" became clear as the flotsam and jetsam began hitting Christie's and Sotheby's. One really didn't "own" anything. You just possessed things over a transitory period during which the Fates smiled down upon you. For the Lehmanites, the riches would prove ephemeral. Now other potential owners were foraging through the stuff like blowfly larvae.

Before the decaying edifice came crashing down, Lehmanites would gather to discuss their day-to-day woes at watering holes like the Rose Bar at the Gramercy Park Hotel.

There, investment bankers grumbled about the pressure to line up summer rentals in the Hamptons by Presidents' Day and the unceasing struggle of finding a good fill-in nanny on the regular nanny's day off. There was also the eternal drama of getting your kids in the right schools that promised the right level of social anointment.

"Once you moved to Greenwich, even the public schools were terrific, [but] everyone ended up wanting to be at Greenwich Academy or Brunswick, which meant ultimately the same application nightmare there," wrote Alexandra Lebenthal in the "Recessionistas," the author's 2010 farce about Manhattan's coddled elite during the Great Recession.

"The fact is that some people would gladly pay $30,000 a year to have their kids at the right schools with the right people rather than get an equally good free education at a public school.

"The universal thing about having money," wrote Lebenthal, "is that no matter how much you have, it isn't enough."

Working moms on the Upper East Side were rare, she

observed. For many women, it simply didn't pencil. "What was the point of making $200,000 when her spouse could be making $10 million?" Plus, you, as a wage slave, would have to put up with the antics of a horde of middle-class strivers simply to claim your measly $200,000.

In a January 2017 study in the journal Nature Communications, researchers Lena Grinsted and Jeremy Field, both at the University of Sussex in the United Kingdom, monitored paper wasp mothers as they recruited wasp "au pairs" to live in the hive and help out with chores. The wasp moms laid the eggs and then buzzed the hive's social circuit, while their au pair governesses cared for the offspring. The latter were also expected to help build out the nest and forage, but the deal was essentially a housing-for-childcare trade.

Upon closer inspection, though, the principle of supply and demand was found to shape the conditions of the nannies' arrangement. Socialite Grigsby Somerset and her investment banker husband, Blake, protagonists in Lebenthal's fictional romp, would have been equipped to predict this part right off. When researchers increased the number of nests in the field, they discovered the wasp moms were willing to accept smaller contributions from their helpers. The researchers artificially created a hot market for nannies when they introduced additional needy moms into the mix.

The wasp moms behaved like any rent-seeking user of domestic help in Beverly Hills, Palm Beach, Belle Meade or Buckhead by offering more advantageous terms and conditions for the exchange when demand for the nannies increased.

The greater supply of wasp nests lowered the price of entry into any single nest.

"A bad deal is better than no deal," Grinsted told the Independent. "So, when competition increases so does the risk that you have to accept a lower price for what you offer."

Lehman seemed to always show a prowess for maneuvering through economic wipeouts and upheavals – an unlucky exposure to any one of which could have brought the investment bank down.

In the 1930s, Lehman underwrote the initial public offering of the pioneering television maker DuMont Laboratories with its cathode-ray tube, which would become the TV screen, and its Orwellian-sounding "magic eye" tuning tube. It also underwrote big players in the oil-field services industry and, in the 1950s, it financed the computing revolution with its initial public offering of Digital Equipment Corporation.

In its century-and-a-half, Lehman weathered the Civil War; the railroad boom-and-bust cycles of the late 1800s; the bank panics of the 1890s and the aughts; the Great Depression; two world wars; the junk-bond collapse of the late 1980s, which culminated in the destruction of Drexel Burnham; a capital shortage after its 1994 spinoff from American Express; the 1998 fall of Long-Term Capital Management, which did business with nearly every big firm on Wall Street; and the dot-com bust of 2000 to 2002.

Who would have guessed something as banal as the U.S. housing market would have taken it down?

***

When Lehman gave up its ghost, a reality quickly set in among its employees that this would not be like being downsized or fired for cause. There would be no severance, no share value, no healthcare, no salary and no negotiating.

But the bolt-from-the-blue job losses at Lehman were but one part of it. The potential loss of social stature and the ensuing class abandonment – and the hideous ridicule or pity that might come with this – could prove equally unbearable as any descent from affluence to destitution.

Nineteenth century German sociologist Max Weber summed it up in his Theory of Status Groups – communities based on ideas of lifestyle and honor that groups assert. Members in status groups, according to Weber, are pressured to engage with people of like status and there are big limitations on social intercourse outside the caste.

In certain ancient Egyptian murals, the relative social ranking of the figures was conveyed by their size in the mural itself. These erstwhile towering figures were now at risk of shrinking in their own murals.

Living in reduced circumstances, Lehmanites could quietly curtail shopping trips, restaurant visits and the April-in-Paris excursions. The personal trainer could go but not the nanny. Also, this was September. The kids couldn't rightly be yanked from school at the beginning of the school year.

Ousted the same day as Gregory was Erin Callan, Lehman's rock star chief financial officer and Gregory protégée. Her fall to Earth was rivaled only by her meteoric ascendence to Club 31. She had become Lehman's "Grrrl Power" icon. She helmed the bank's rear-guard action in a vicious heel-biting campaign from the stop-at-nothing short-seller and Lehman arch-nemesis David Einhorn. After leaving Lehman, she took a job at Credit Suisse and then took a leave of absence.

Like the nomadic Matthew Lee, who was witnessed riding through one-horse sheep stations in Australia's Outback, Callan herself became Greta Garbo-like.

In August 2009, her attorney declined repeated requests for comment, but people who knew her told CNBC that the intense stress from the Lehman disaster was one reason she didn't return to work. She was reported to have withdrawn to a wood-shingled house in East Hampton, going to spin classes at a local gym and dating a fireman.

One hundred and fifty thousand square feet of light-emitting diode screens "wrapped" the exterior base of the Lehman tower. The weekend the investment bank was struck by misfortune, it displayed spectacular blue ocean, with waves pummeling a rocky shoreline, creating brilliant white spumes in the impact zone. The display was an icon of the gleaming tower at 745 Seventh Avenue in the middle of the throbbing metropolis. The LED display was the largest in the world at the time of its completion. The imagery was accompanied by the slogan "Where vision gets built."

"[The slogan] is something none of us ever understood," admitted Lynn Gray, Lehman's then-Global Chief Administrative Officer a decade later. How could a vision be *built*? It no doubt gave rise to many a sardonic argument between off-duty traders in the bombastic velvet armchairs of the Rose Bar.

"Isn't a finished product built from a vision? Isn't the vision something that *comes* to you? Shouldn't it be more like, 'Where the vision *materializes*' or, 'Where the vision is *realized*'?"

"No, no, no. The vision has to be *crafted*. The client most of the time doesn't *have* a vision."

"I'm sorry – the vision is the *vision*. Where's the authenticity of the vision if it has to be synthesized by mad scientists at a global investment banking firm? The vision isn't "*built*," for God's sake!"

Anyway, this type of banal tagline was interchangeable with many others of the era.

In October 2001, Lehman had purchased the 37-story, million-square-foot tower, designed by the New York firm Kohn, Pedersen, and Fox, for $700 million. The building had recently been completed, but not yet occupied, by rival Morgan Stanley. Lehman was looking for a new global headquarters after Three World Financial Center was damaged in the attacks of 9-11.

Fuld's private dining room, with its rich mahogany joinery and gadrooned silver tea service, was one floor up from Club 31.

In September 2009, about a year after Lehman had given up the ghost, a rearguard of 600 financial staff and consultants with the firm Alvarez & Marsal – known in bankruptcy circles as "A&M" – picked over Lehman's corpse on the 45th Floor of the Time-Life Building on Sixth Avenue and 51st Street. They unwound millions of derivatives contracts, paid tax liabilities and processed creditor claims.

Tony Lomas, chairman of PricewaterhouseCoopers' Business Recovery Services unit in Europe, and once the bankruptcy administrator of Enron's European arm, was joint administrator of Lehman Brothers in Europe. He was quoted in the Sunday Times as saying the Lehman case had "become an industry in itself" and its wind-down would generate more than $4 billion in fees for about 2,000 people globally.

In October, the first 280 pieces of artwork and ephemera, most from the Lehman Building's 31st and 32nd floors, went under the hammer at an auction house in Philadelphia. The sale was the first of three lots totaling 400 pieces to be flogged off.

The contemporary works included the photograph, "New York Mercantile Exchange 1991" by the German photographer Andreas Gursky and Gary Hume's "Madonna" – once described by a critic as "disconcertingly featureless." Hume is best-known for his minimalist depictions of everyday objects using high-gloss industrial paint. "The edge is the only thing that matters," he once said of his paintings.

There was "Head of Bruce Bernard," a signed etching by the British portraitist Lucian Freud and "The White Hyacinth" by Mary Fedden.

It's not unusual for banks to build enormous art collections. They hold artwork as investments and as status symbols, but mostly the latter in a competition for the idealized stature of the modern-day Medici.

Swiss bank UBS was once reported to own 40,000 works of art while JPMorgan Chase was said to hold a 30,000-strong collection. Future generations will no doubt be hard-pressed to make sense of it all.

During the great unwinding of Lehman, the bank also disgorged works of the Old Masters, including "The Ship Frankfield off Table Bay" by Samuel Walters; The "Mare Dolly with Jockey; a Race Beyond" by the renowned sporting artist Francis Sartorius; and "A Frigate in Three Positions off the Dover Coast" by Thomas Luny.

There was also the obligatory assortment of silver tea caddies; rare cigar boxes; Chinese ceramics; and leather-bound books, including the works of Charles Dickens, Samuel Johnson and William Shakespeare.

The fallen alpha pair Dick and Kathy Fuld were prominent patrons of the arts in their own right. Kathy donated or otherwise helped acquire 42 pieces for the Museum of Modern Art. She collected Cy Twombly, Brice Marden and Jasper Johns. In 2002 she joined the museum's board and by 2007 was a vice-chairman. A gallery was named after the couple. An appointment to the MoMA board was a one-shot social climb into high-Earth orbit. No one would be writing off Kathy Fuld as a wealthy dabbler.

MoMA honored Dick Fuld with the David Rockefeller award for "enlightened generosity and advocacy of cultural and civic endeavors" in February 2006. His acceptance speech, one attendee told the New York Times, was revelatory about his true interest in abstract expressionism: "Kathy loves modern art and I love Kathy."

MoMA was looking for enlightened advocacy. It got honesty instead. Dick Fuld, its great benefactor, seemingly had no interest in the promiscuous squiggles of a Brice Marden or the angry, frantic scrawls of a Cy Twombly.

Nonetheless, Fuld would get after-hours access to the museum itself and bring in a hundred or so newly minted Lehman managing directors and senior executives and their spouses. For attendees, it was social ecstasy. It was a place where things were happening. You could see it from the phalanx of hired town cars pulling past the main entrance of the Rockefeller Building on 53rd Street.

The last traces of evening daylight poured into MoMA's Marron Atrium and suffused the Lehmanites at the 40-odd tables, each seating 10 guests, with a glorious amber glow. Even the museum's checkroom could be sublime with social kisses and transfixed conversations.

In the rapturous meet-and-greet portion amid the gloaming, small groups clustered in the collection galleries and the sculpture garden. It was like church, but with the air tinctured with the smell of freshly printed banknotes.

These events were a sea of radiant shoulders and spaghetti straps and flashes of gold-and-onyx cuff links and buzzing social clusters. There were peals of collegial laughter sprinkled, occasionally, with accented English and foreign tongues. Was that Estonian? There were social grins and spasms of repartee and exquisite musings. A few swells, their backs deferentially hunched, groveled to make eye contact with the supremo. Just to lock on to Fuld's laser beams, to exchange an amused or knowing look with the generalissimo, was like having a brief backchannel to the godhead.

The Lehman wives were starved to perfection and poured into everything from simple black frocks to eveningwear smocked with gold thread. The Lehman wives always seemed to have impeccable posture.

At events like these, Fuld was known to summon up Ares, the god of war. In Fuld's worldview, Lehman employees were combatants in a savage struggle; Fuld personified the physical aggression required to be triumphant on the field of battle. Under his generalship, Lehmanites would gird their loins and smite their foes, bite off their heads and eat their livers whole. He would talk of "ripping out the still-beating hearts" of the bank's adversaries.

The Lehmanites drank in the ice-veined martinet's exhortations like newly indoctrinated Viet Cong. Even the new Lehman wives got on board. Just like that, they, too, sitting next to their foot soldiers, were along for the psychodrama. Just like that, they displayed a degree of bloodlust not frequently seen within the walls of MoMA. But such was the gladiatorial ethos at the House of Lehman.

The irony was that these events at MoMA could easily have been pieces of performance art themselves, sprouted from the mind of a Marina Abramović or a Carolee Schneemann. The art could have been presented to the public, or, still better, made immersive, *involving* the public, putting each observer in the place of an attendee in a meticulously set-designed space, complete with gustatory touches like salmon sashimi squares drizzled with yuzu basil oil and barrel-aged balsamic. Some of the MoMA trustees would have loved it; others would have winced. It might have hit a little too close to home.

In those heady days, the museum had just undergone a $425 million renovation by the then-largely unknown Japanese architect Yoshio Taniguchi. In the "visioning" phase for the renovation, the trustees spent three weeks aboard Ron Lauder's jet. He of the Estée Lauder fortune. They combed the world's museums. They flew first to Europe, then around the United States and then to Asia. Video artist Bill Viola wanted the remodel to accommodate new forms of art — to no one's surprise, video art – but also forms that hadn't been invented yet. A portentous thought was uttered to the New Yorker by MoMA director Glenn Lowry: "What is contemporary today is going to become historical at some point in the not-too-distant future. Then you have the dilemma – where is the line?"

Now Fuld, Lehman's maximum leader, with privileges to MoMA – you never said "*the* MoMA," only "MoMA" – was exhorting young Lehman executives to rip the hearts out of their freshly slain enemies and eat them. It wasn't about simmering the enemies' organ meats in celery stalks, scallions, juniper berries and beer from an old-timey chuck wagon at base camp. This was biting into the warm, fast-twitch muscle and stealing some poor bastard's warrior spirit right there where he fell.

Some attributed Fuld's bellicosity to the so-called Avis Effect – Lehman was only the nation's fourth-largest investment bank. It had to try harder. If that meant exhorting his people to rip out their enemies' beating hearts and eat the god-damned things while they were still trying to pump blood, then so be it.

 Less than a month after Lehman's collapse, Kathy Fuld was conspicuously absent from a dinner for the museum's new top curator. It didn't escape the notice of the society columnists, who were already craning to see how the Wall Street unpleasantness might be affecting the MoMA benefactress. It was like British tabloid journalists in 1954 trying to spy whether Prince Charles had, in fact, lost a baby tooth. You had to be somewhat subtle as you craned and gawked at the tiny royal's maw.

Kathy Fuld often shared the head table at such functions with MoMA heavyweights like Lowry, but that afternoon her husband was in D.C. testifying before Congress, reported New York magazine.

MoMA was silent about the no-show. "We don't comment on the whereabouts of our trustees," said the museum in a terse statement.

In the wake of the Lehman collapse, the Fulds sold off a personal collection of abstract impressionist drawings, including three by Willem de Kooning. A shockwavelet from the troubles on Wall Street even hit the auction house Christie's, which was reported to have given the Fulds a $20 million guarantee on 16 postwar drawings, including the three by de Kooning, but the lot only fetched $13.5 million.

Like the Fulds, Joe and Niki Gregory began auctioning off a collection of centuries-old furniture and artwork from the Lloyd Harbor place. In September 2013, Sotheby's announced "important English furniture from some of the most notable cabinetmakers, along with European porcelain and decorations" would be auctioned off.

Among the items listed for auction were two 18th century commodes, with an estimated value of $120,000 and $400,000, and a painting by the Dutch artist Bartholomeus Assteyn with the tortuous title "A Still Life of Grapes, Cherries, Peaches and Other Fruit in a Basket, with a Rose and a Dragonfly on a Stone Ledge," listed for between $60,000 and $80,000.

Author McDonald believes senior executives' penchant for expensive art was a result of "becoming consumed with legacy, with power and with projection of power."

Then there was the sale of Lehman's two Gulfstream IVs

– known as "G-Fours" – hangared at the Westchester County Airport in White Plains, New York, convenient for Fuld, who lived in nearby Greenwich, Connecticut. The aircraft, each powered by two Rolls-Royce RB.183 Tay turbofans, could carry 15 Lehmanites and their guests and a profusion of Italian leather valises, Filson twill duffles, skis, snowboards, golf bags, flyrods and float tubes above the weather, and across countries and oceans.

From tarmacs at Teterboro, White Plains, Ft. Lauderdale, Phoenix Deer Valley and Van Nuys, members of the Lumpenproletariat – low-rent techies, hedgies and celebutants – gawped yearningly from their Hawkers, Citations and other flying tubes that made you walk hunchbacked around the cabin and detour around weather. If you had one of these light business jets, your pilots would always be sweating takeoff-abort scenarios. Everyone knew this.

But the muscular G-Fours were something else. They allowed Lehmanites to climb out at 4,000 feet per minute – at 61.5 kilonewtons! – and cruise at almost 500 miles an hour, *above* the weather. Ascending into the heavens at 61.5 kilonewtons was like getting a massage covering every nerve ending of the body. All the while, Lehmanites were cocooned in a cabin with sumptuous etched-glass dividers, retractable cabin monitors, sound-dampening doors, a full-service galley and wet bar, and more than 6-feet-2 inches of headroom.

So long as you weren't in someplace like Kathmandu, the beast could outclimb virtually any mountain if an engine failed on takeoff. Also, if you sufficiently charmed your pilots, they might take the ship above its recommended ceiling. You could see the curvature of the Earth and touch the whiskers of God! The thing was a gas hog, but fuel burn was never an issue at Lehman. Besides, with a decent tailwind, you could aviate from Van Nuys to Teterboro in under four hours.

One of the conveyances had recently ferried Fuld lieutenant Tom Russo to Seoul to discuss a potential $5 billion strategic investment from the Korean Development Bank during Lehman's attempt in 2008 to find a buyer for itself.

When Bear Stearns failed, Fuld was en route on one of the ships to India to meet clients. The G-Fours, which were Fuld's ex officio, often ferried the maximum leader to his home in Jupiter, Florida; and the 71-acre spread in Sun Valley, with its Hermann Göring fireplaces and private trout stream.

A Dassault Falcon 50 and a Sikorsky helicopter were also hawked in the wake of Lehman's collapse. In October 2009, the last of Lehman's corporate aircraft went under the gavel – a Gulfstream 550 purchased for about $40 million in 2006. The investment bank had never used it. Lehman raised almost $90 million from selling the planes and helicopter, or roughly 97 cents to the dollar of their book value.

The shockwave brought on by the disintegration of Lehman meant bank holding companies would soon be carpet-bombed with new regulations and policy prescriptions.

New compliance burdens would punish small banks disproportionately, and trigger new spasms of consolidation and with it, fewer choices and higher costs.

Bit by bit, almost imperceptibly, regulation has steadily depleted consumer choice in retail banking. Trends in bank charters were already showing consolidation since the late 1980s. Now, the Treasury and Fed would be picking winners and losers as never before. Consumers and small businesses – the great drivers of the economy – would be at the mercy of the "cleaner wrasses."

The cleaner wrasse is a fish that provides tooth- and scale-cleaning services to big open-ocean carnivores like the barracuda with little risk of being eaten. Each wrasse has an "office" on a piece of coral. "Clients," like the barracuda, come by for a cleaning. The wrasse occasionally sneaks a morsal or two of living tissue or protective mucus off the client – call it a "junk fee." Too many of these junk fees, and the client will swim away. Some clients are forced to wait longer for a servicing, while others are served right away.

The kinds of monopolistic abuses that occur from bank consolidation are no doubt something Redouan Bshary, a professor of behavioral ecology at the University of Neuchâtel in Switzerland, could discuss in great detail. Consolidation helps explain the differences in service quality provided by the cleaner wrasse, a fish Bshary studies.

Bshary found that fish that had the ability to swim longer distances – that is, shop a greater number of cleaner wrasses – almost always received faster service and gentler treatment. He also found that those same clients preferred cleanings by wrasses working in two-fish teams, and those clients usually got their way.

The pitiable customers who couldn't range as far were over a barrel. The wrasses somehow sensed this. The locals were made to wait longer for a cleaning and were much more likely to lose live tissue and mucus in add-on fees. The big fish had somehow reached a modus vivendi with the wrasses. To paraphrase the 18th century economist Adam Smith, "Monopolists, you suck mucus!"

"It's just amazing how sophisticated [the wrasses'] decision routes are," said Bshary to a science writer.

The Lehman bankruptcy would, in fact, unleash a regulatory storm, and the local yokels – the small fish – would bear the brunt of it in extra costs and fewer choices.

In the enormous gyre of Lehman assets being picked through by accountants was 500,000 pounds of yellowcake uranium – an unenriched form of the metal – in a secure storage facility in Canada, which Bloomberg News described as nearly enough for a nuclear bomb or to fuel a nuclear reactor for one year. Lehman had begun trading in uranium futures, and during the chaos of the bankruptcy had not settled the contract. It ended up taking delivery of the stuff. This sent liquidators on a months-long odyssey of trying to offload the commodity.

At the glass-and-steel tower on the million-windowed island virtually no trace of Lehman remains save for one element: Just above the ground floor, the names of world cities set in steel in a Futura typeface – San Francisco, New York, Hong Kong, Tokyo, Madrid, Chicago, Frankfurt, London – remain. During the Lehman era, they corresponded to the major worldwide offices of the investment bank.

Lehman's slide into the Halusian Gulp, as author Tom Wolfe would have put it, was the product of a culture that rewarded risk-taking over risk mitigation and a rigid chain of command that kept employees from sharing bad news with their bosses – those cocooned in Club 31.

A week after Lehman Weekend, Fuld was reportedly on a treadmill at his gym when a man walked over and punched him, knocking him out cold.

Two weeks later, Fuld became the national poster child and chief villain for Wall Street's excesses when the 110th Congress summoned him to Washington to testify before the House Committee on Oversight and Government Reform. Congress would finally get a snootful of the Repo 105 and the scales would fall from their eyes. But that was not to be.

The major focus of the hearing was executive compensation, including Fuld's. It seemed more designed to fan the flames of resentment rather than probe the causes of the nation's largest bankruptcy. First, the embers of public outrage had to be properly stoked. Maybe that would be the extent of the whole thing. And, besides, Congress hadn't yet heard of the Repo 105.

The firm, in the days before it filed for bankruptcy, sought board approval to pay three departing executives more than $20 million, earning the opprobrium of the committee chair, U.S. Representative Henry Waxman of California.

"Even as Mr. Fuld was pleading for a federal rescue, Lehman continued to squander millions on executive compensation," snapped Waxman during the subcommittee hearing.

The congressman unveiled a chart showing what he said was $480 million in compensation that had gone to Fuld since 2000.

"Your company is now bankrupt and our country is in a state of crisis – but you get to keep $480 million," said Waxman. "I have a very basic question for you: Is that fair?"

The congressman was now treating Fuld like a disobedient child. His question didn't invite debate but it did elicit a stimulus-response bond. Fuld squirmed slightly, removed his glasses and looked away. After a pause, he muttered something dejectedly about some of his compensation being in stock options.

Waxman soldiered on, pointing out that Fuld owned a $14 million oceanfront home in Florida, a $14 million Park Avenue flat, another home in Sun Valley, Idaho, and an art collection.

Fuld was just going to ride this out.

"I would say to you the [$500 million] number is not accurate. I believe the amount that I took out of the company is a little bit over $250 million," bristled Fuld. To Waxman, it was a distinction without a difference.

Lawmakers were still catching flak from constituents from a vote the week earlier authorizing the largest federal bailout in history.

House Republicans dismissed the hearing as little more than Kabuki theater, since the committee refused to examine Fannie Mae and Freddie Mac's involvement in the financial crisis.

"If you haven't discovered your role, you're the villain today," Representative John Mica of Florida told Fuld, flashing him a conspiratorial smirk, that all but said, "Brother, you and I understand what's going on here, right?"

Fuld acknowledged the remark, his mouth arranging itself in a mirthless smile.

House minority leader John Boehner of Ohio, also a Republican, accused Waxman of refusing to investigate Freddie and Fannie "solely to shield his fellow Democrats politically," and said it "cheats the American people of key facts that could help all of us learn how we got here – and what we must do to make certain this situation never repeats itself."

Fuld attributed Lehman's collapse to poor regulation, short-sellers like Lehman arch-villain and unwavering antipode David Einhorn of Greenlight Capital and a "financial tsunami" that engulfed Lehman. But to Waxman, it was the Reichstag Fire explanation.

Fuld may have been a true believer, right to the bitter end. He reportedly kept 10 million shares and lost almost $1 billion. Meanwhile, three sets of prosecutors had launched probes, looking into whether Lehman shareholders had been duped.

On Monday, September 15, 2008, there was a constant ringing of phones on all floors of the Lehman Building. It was eerie. When Lehman's analysts, executive assistants, attorneys, paralegals, associates, account managers, vice presidents, directors and managing directors all left the building the

Friday before, they whistled past the graveyard, believing Bank of America or Barclays would scoop up Lehman over the weekend.

On Sunday evening, about the time Lehman lawyers were filling out the bankruptcy papers, the tower was disgorging mostly younger males in ball caps, ratty T-shirts and flip-flops. A few emerged in crisp golf shirts and plaid shorts. The tang of fall was not yet in the air. All carried bankers boxes or had daypacks slung over their shoulders. If you were a Lehman employee and you wanted to experience the carnage firsthand, you headed to 745 Seventh Avenue. Some were simply retrieving their stuff.

"We [were] told there was a possibility we might not have access to the building the next day," said Grimeh, the polo-shirted one who had thrown up the Churchillian "V"-for-victory sign and been canonized by the media – he whose image had been raised as the very icon of the Lehman collapse. He told the Wall Street Journal that he was amazed at the number of shoes women at the firm kept under their desks.

A crush of humanity streamed into the building that Sunday afternoon. A trio of security guards, dressed in the non-confrontational "concierge look," stood beside polished stainless-steel bollards at the building's entrance. They looked at badges as employees threaded their way into the tower's main concourse.

The Hudson was slate-blue. Tourists seemed less interested in the growing media presence around the building. They seemed to fixate on the general hubbub of the metropolis – Times Square! What was happening? We've heard so much about the Naked Cowboy! Where was the Naked Cowboy?

"Excuse me, sir! How are you feeling?" a voice yelled out from a mob of shabbily dressed, mostly white people. Their upturned faces had "voyeur" written all over them. Reporters!

"I don't know," said a pale, freckled man in his 20s who had just emerged from the Lehman building. He blushed a deep crimson. "What do *you* think? This was my first week on the job."

Sunbursts exploded and camera shutters clicked in quick succession. An intense video floodlight now shone in the young man's eyes. He squinted into the sunbursts and the glare.

For the reporters, this was manna from heaven. A small swarm broke out from the larger swarm and encircled the man – he who had worked one week on the job. A man with washed-out blue eyes shoved a bony white hand containing a digital recorder about an inch from the young man's face.

"Who is *he*?" asked a woman in a gravelly, smoke-cured voice. Next to her was a heavy-set woman with close-cropped hair in a safari jacket with pockets everywhere. She was snapping away on an SLR camera that seemed to be attached to her face like a proboscis. Slung across her shoulder was a second camera mounted on an enormous telescopic lens.

"Dunno. It was his first week on the job…" said a man's voice in an outer-borough dialect.

"No kiddin'?" said another man. "Well, he just got the surprise of his young life."

And so it was. When an employee carrying a bankers box emerged from the revolving glass door at the building's concourse, the swarm would train their cameras on that person. If the person so much as uttered a single syllable – or even acknowledged the swarm – a dozen sunbursts exploded off the cameras.

A twentysomething in shirt-sleeves hefting a bankers box tied with a piece of string walked hurriedly along Seventh Avenue. He was followed by a short, sallow-faced man in a

Mets warm-up jacket and disheveled hair. Beside him was an overweight black man in cargo shorts, tube socks and a guayabera shirt stretched taut over his torso like a sausage casing. A large Sony video camera seemed to be growing out of the fat man's shoulder and the orbital cavity of his right eye. The man's eye was furiously mingled with the camera's eye piece. With singular determination, the glass eye watched the man carrying the bankers box.

Earlier that Sunday, more than 25,000 people had lined up in Central Park West before 9:20 a.m. for the 2008 Komen NYC Race for the Cure. When word got out about the situation at Lehman, the TV vans covering the largely ho-hum event began converging on Seventh Avenue opposite the Lehman building, the antenna shaft of each one, each wrapped in a helix of coiled cable, began telescoping skyward with a mechanical humming sound as onlookers gawked.

Some Lehman employees emerged from the building with moist eyes. Most left the building quietly and declined interviews. By now, reporters and a few onlookers were behind a police barricade that had suddenly gone up. They waited, resting on one foot then the other.

This time, another man in his 20s emerged from the edifice and erupted at the scrum.

"Are you enjoying this? he yelled. "You think this is funny?" His eyelids fluttered uncontrollably.

The faces of the reporters now livened up with the unmistakably satisfied smiles ... of ... *schadenfreude*. Yes, it was now funny only because the man had screamed at members of the Fourth Estate, asking them if they thought it was funny. It was a self-fulfilling prophecy.

A few of the younger, more brazen employees liberated Lehman Brothers swag from the place, including any kind of Lehman Brothers signage they could haul away. "Where vision gets built" read one boosted placard. It seemed like a fitting end.

The Lehman Weekend was the watershed event of the U.S. subprime financial crisis that circled the globe like a contagion in 2008. Lehman's collapse did much to trigger the evaporation of close to $10 trillion in capitalization from global equity markets in October, which saw their largest monthly decline on record at the time.

What destroyed Lehman was greed, hubris and something economists call "moral hazard" – a lack of incentive to guard against risk where one feels protected from its consequences. Later, some called this sense of being insulated from risk a "too big to fail" mentality. Lehman's blunder into the subprime mortgage market was its Siren song – not to mention its swan song.

At first, Lehman's mortgage-backed acquisitions looked nothing short of brilliant. Revenue from its real estate businesses grew Lehman's capital-markets unit by 56 percent from 2004 to 2006. Those in Lehman's investment-banking and asset-management divisions looked on in awe. In 2007, the firm reported net income of a record $4.2 billion on revenues of $19.3 billion. In the second quarter of that year alone, Lehman reported its profits had surged 27 percent, a record for the firm, with net income of $1.3 billion that quarter, topping the $1 billion it had earned in the period a year earlier.

In February 2007, Lehman shares reached their perihelion at $86.18.

But later that quarter, cracks in the U.S. housing market emerged. In March, the stock market saw its biggest single-day plunge in five years, while the number of subprime mortgage defaults rose to a seven-year high.

In a conference call, Lehman announced the risks posed

by rising home delinquencies were well contained and would have little impact on Lehman's earnings. It didn't anticipate problems in the subprime market that would affect the rest of the housing market or damage the U.S. economy.

In August that year, BNP Paribas, France's largest publicly traded bank, announced it was barring investors from redeeming $2.2 billion, citing U.S. subprime mortgage woes. It was the start of the worst financial convulsion since the 1930s.

That month, Lehman cut 1,200 mortgage-related jobs and shuttered its BNC Mortgage unit. It also closed offices of Alt-A lender Aurora in three states. The month ended with the failure of Ameriquest, the largest subprime lender in the United States.

But Lehman's underwriting spigot was still wide open. Like a ravenous Paramecium, the investment bank was still feeding on job lots of subprime mortgages and creating mortgage-backed securities and their derivatives, underwriting more of them in 2007 than any other Wall Street firm, amassing an $85 billion portfolio, or four times shareholder equity. All the while, the subprime mortgages – the underlying assets – were unraveling. Its heavy leverage and enormous mortgage-securities portfolio made it uniquely vulnerable. A year earlier, Lehman had been the nation's No. 1 underwriter of securities backed by subprime mortgages.

In October 2007, the New York Times ran a feature on Lehman Brothers titled "The Survivor." Lehman insiders reminisced about "the ugly days of August," as if the crisis had been averted.

On March 17, 2008, the day after Bear Stearns' implosion and JPMorgan's $2-a-share purchase of its brokerage assets, Lehman saw its shares plummet by nearly 40 percent in early trading. Investors shuddered at what might be on Lehman's balance sheets, and the ranks of potential bailout partners were drawing thin.

In his book "Bailout Nation," author Barry Ritholtz describes how Fuld squandered Lehman's best opportunity to secure funding after Bear Stearns imploded. Warren Buffett came round and offered to take a stake in Lehman. Buffett's Berkshire Hathaway offered to buy preferred shares that would pay a dividend of 9 percent and could be converted to common stock at the then-market price of $40.30.

"Although this deal may have been pricier than any others," wrote Ritholtz, "it had two advantages: it was real, and the imprimatur of the world's most respected investor might have guaranteed Lehman's survival."

Fuld spurned Buffett's offer. It was a kamikaze move.

Buffett later went to Goldman Sachs, where he got a better deal: $5 billion in preferred Goldman stock with a dividend of 10 percent. Buffett also wrangled warrants to buy another $5 billion in common stock over five years at a strike price of $115 a share.

Like other Wall Street firms, Lehman was engaging in so-called "staple financing" – acquisition deals in which it played both sides of a sale, earning one fee for its advisory services to the seller while it earned other fees by providing financing to the potential buyer. This created a conflict of interest, since sellers and their counselors hold out for the highest price, while buyers, and their financiers, negotiate for the lowest price. It muddied the bank's motivations.

Lehman stock plummeted 77 percent in the first week of September 2008.

Over the summer, Lehman's management had made a number of failed gambits to attract potential partners. There was Russo's trip to Seoul to make representations to the Korean Development Bank.

"Fuld had posted a discreet 'For Sale' sign on his firm as early as last spring," wrote author Michael M. Thomas. "Back then, the credit crisis was but a mote in Mammon's eye. And yet Fuld found no takers. Why? Why did one potential buyer after another – banks and investment banks from Wall Street to Beijing, sovereign funds, you name it – take a sniff and fade away? What did they see?"

Hopes that the Korea Development Bank would take a stake in Lehman fizzled on September 9, as the state-owned South Korean bank shelved talks.

On Wednesday, September 10, 2008, "We bailed from our classroom in the basement and went up to the trading floor to listen to the quarterly earnings call," wrote the then-newly hired Lehman analyst Alex Sienaert in a retrospective piece in Salon a decade later. "[The earnings call] had been rushed forward ahead of schedule in a doomed attempt to convince the market that the company was going to survive.

"The CFO announced a $3.9 billion quarterly loss, the failure to find an investor willing to inject fresh capital, and the rest was noise. The trading floor fell silent. Even so, some modicum of work continued through the end of that week, even as the company's share price kept sliding."

The rating-agency Moody's announced it would be reviewing Lehman's credit ratings, and it found that the only way for Lehman to avoid a rating downgrade would be to sell a majority stake to a strategic partner. September 11, 2008, saw another massive rout for Lehman shares, which slid 42 percent. Reports surfaced late in the day that the investment bank was trying to find a buyer for the whole firm.

Hedge fund clients began abandoning the company, with short-term creditors following suit.

The feeling of moral hazard was still strong.

"On Friday, September 12, I think most people left the

office assuming that over the weekend, we would find out whether we were going to be purchased by Bank of America or Barclays," Gray, Lehman's then-Global Administrative Officer, told the Wall Street Journal.

But the insouciance quickly ended when it became evident that neither suitor would rescue Lehman.

It's strange what people fixate on in such moments. Odd things ran through employees' minds on Sunday night and Monday morning.

Vending machines and catering services in the Lehman building used a prepaid card system. Sienaert's card balance needed to be spent before the building was shuttered. When he got there, he discovered the vending machines had been emptied of everything but cheese puffs. He also needed to cancel his gym membership in the building.

"The cancellation form required me to fill in my reason. I wrote 'company in liquidation' and added my form to the pile. HR continued to act as though it was business as usual," wrote Sienaert. He described the human-resources reps as being angry at the end.

"Far-removed from the financial front lines of the company, they had had no real clue that the company had been sliding toward bankruptcy for months. They had carried on their staff recruitment and on-boarding duties as normal, and now they felt like fools."

Weeks later, liquidators even clawed back Sienaert's sign-on bonus – with interest.

"When the Fed was debating bailing out Lehman," wrote Ritholtz, "I imagine someone in the room saying: 'These guys rejected capital from Buffett — why should we bail them out if they wouldn't help themselves?'"

Lehman's implosion convulsed global markets for weeks afterward. Many on Wall Street second-guessed the U.S.

government's decision to let Lehman fail, wiping out $46 billion of its market value. Its collapse also played a role in Bank of America's acquisition of Merrill Lynch in an 11th-hour deal that was also announced on September 15.

After his appearances on Capitol Hill, Fuld went largely radio-silent, but a 2015 keynote address at the Marcum MicroCap Conference, touted as Fuld's "first public address since leaving Lehman in 2008," featured the former Lehman chief lamenting to a ballroom of penny-stock promoters that "small companies can't get financing." Bloomberg reported the conference "attracted promoters and hustlers looking to drum up investments in tiny, speculative companies.

Most attendees at the conference in Midtown Manhattan had probably not much contemplated this occasion – Fuld's first big reappearance in public since the fall of Lehman. The attendees weren't exactly the cream of the Knickerbocracy.

"One of Fuld's fellow speakers was a 28-year-old who made a fortune lending money in arrangements known to some as 'death-spiral financing,'" reported Bloomberg. "Other presenters included representatives from a marijuana-centric social network and a nano-medicine company that claims it's onto cures for HIV and Ebola."

Fuld's appearance at the penny-stock show sent up a rather desperate flare. He seemed to be singing for his supper. But he had no hangdog air about him.

"September 2008, we lost the firm," he said. We *lost* the firm. He said it like Uncle Ned at Thanksgiving dinner recounting the loss of Grandma Becky to a virulent strain of pneumonia. He was still critical of the U.S. government.

The Lehman meltdown turned out to be a watershed event in a global economic crisis that is fading from memory, but that period of upheaval altered the U.S. economy and the global financial system.

Nearly $8 trillion in stock-market value was erased between late 2007 and 2009. The shock ushered in the most sweeping stimulus by central banks ever, with zero or negative interest rates; it normalized their purchase of trillions in securities. The economy lost 8.8 million jobs. Collectively, Americans lost $9.8 trillion in wealth as their home values plunged and their retirement accounts cratered.

"It was such a shock to the economic system that it unleashed dynamics that we still don't understand fully," Joe Brusuelas, chief economist at RSM, an audit and advisory firm, told the Washington Post.

The Great Recession ended with a slow-motion recovery that began in July 2009 and lasted 128 months to February 2020. This surpasses the previous record of 120 months from March 1991 to March 2001.

U.S. housing prices peaked in early 2006. By 2009, foreclosure documents had been filed on 2.8 million properties. More than 2.2 percent of all households were in some stage of foreclosure that year. In Nevada, more than 10 percent of housing units received at least one foreclosure filing in 2009. Arizona saw the nation's second-highest state foreclosure rate the same year, with more than 6 percent of its housing units receiving at least one foreclosure filing.

The San Francisco Fed calculated the disruption, due to a combination of lost work time and lost productivity, had a present-discounted value of about $70,000 for every American.

It took a year for a court-appointed examiner to finish his report on the collapse of Lehman Brothers. The nine-volume, 2,200 page report became the definitive account of the largest bankruptcy in U.S. history.

Fuld and other former top Lehman officials were defendants in multiple civil lawsuits. In exhaustive detail,

Lehman's court-appointed bankruptcy examiner Anton Valukas described how the Repo 105 was used to park assets off Lehman's books to make its end-of-quarter debt seem better than it was.

His voluminous report seized on the Repo 105 as a way to prove the bank had engineered fraudulent transactions, leading to its collapse. But Fuld professed to know nothing of the Repo 105. No Lehmanite was ever perp-walked past fevered citizenry. Certainly none landed on Rikers Island or was sent to some other penal palazzo like one of those fabled "Club Fed" minimum-security facilities with the tennis courts and cardio machines.

When the Repo 105 device was first proposed, Lehman's outside legal counsel no doubt recoiled because of the sheer vileness of the thing. No U.S. law firm, it was reported, would allow the bank to classify repurchase agreements as "sales."

Then Lehman executives discovered Linklaters, an elite British law firm and member of the United Kingdom's revered Magic Circle of law firms. Somehow Linklaters provided Lehman the protective camouflage required for its executives to shift billions back and forth across the Atlantic, making the bank appear healthier than it was. So, the accounting jujitsu was conducted in London through Lehman's European arm. Problem solved.

The report stopped short of suggesting Linklaters had acted illegally or unethically.

A financial services lawyer at another leading London firm told the Financial Times in 2010 that while Linklaters was in a "delicate situation," its behavior was not unusual or ill-judged, as it was most likely one of many law firms that had acted for Lehman over the years.

A casual observer might also gaze upon the actions of auditor Ernst & Young, which certified Lehman's financial statements despite being seemingly handed a roadmap of accounting improprieties from whistleblower Matthew Lee, and conclude Ernst & Young was benefiting from a payola arrangement in which Lehman's handsome fees took precedence over ethics.

But, according to an Ernst & Young spokesman, that casual observer would be wrong. The firm, the spokesman said, stood by its work for 2007, the last year it conducted an audit of Lehman's financial results. Ernst & Young was later sued by New York State in the aiding and abetting of fraud.

In 2010, the Wall Street Journal reported a group of 18 banks — which included Goldman Sachs Group Inc., Morgan Stanley, JPMorgan Chase, Bank of America and Citigroup — had understated their debt levels used to fund securities trades by lowering them an average of 42 percent at the end of each of five consecutive quarterly periods. The banks, which release debt data each quarter, then boosted the debt levels in the middle of successive quarters.

This didn't stop executives at other Wall Street banks from professing surprise at Lehman's accounting tactics.

In 2015, ending a four-year-old lawsuit, Ernst & Young agreed to pay $10 million to settle claims made by the State of New York.

The proceeds went to both Lehman investors and the state. It was much less than the roughly $150 million the state had hoped to recover when the lawsuit was filed.

Lynn E. Turner, a former chief accountant for the Securities and Exchange Commission, accused Ernst & Young of abdicating its responsibility to the audit committee of Lehman's board by not presenting whistleblower concerns.

"This is pretty aggressive and pretty abusive, Turner told the New York Times. "I don't know how under GAAP this follows the rules whatsoever," he said, referring to the

Generally Accepted Accounting Principles.

"That reeks of an auditor who, rather than being really truly independent, is beholden to management," he said, adding that the Securities and Exchange Commission and the Justice Department should follow up on Valukas's findings.

A senior auditor at a Big Three accounting firm, speaking on the condition of anonymity, contends the Repo 105 amounted to not much more than window dressing and was not the reason Lehman failed.

Wharton finance professor Richard Herring puts the responsibility for the abuse of the Repo 105 at the doorstep of Ernst & Young. "[Ernst & Young's] main role was to help the firm misrepresent its actual position to the public," Herring said, noting that reforms after the Enron collapse of 2001 have apparently failed to make accountants the watchdogs they should be.

"It was clearly a dodge…. to circumvent the rules, to try to move things off the balance sheet," wrote Herring's colleague Brian Bushee, a professor of accounting, also at Wharton, of the Repo 105 transactions. "Usually, in these kinds of situations, I try to find some silver lining for the company, to say that there are some legitimate reasons to do this … but it clearly was to get assets off the balance sheet."

Similar to other repos (short for "repurchase agreements"), the Repo 105's mechanics mirrors that of a short-term loan. Valukas's report noted that "Repos generally cannot be treated as sales in the United States because lawyers cannot provide a true sale opinion under U.S. law."

So, Lehman took its chances on English law as applied by the English courts and it found what it liked with the aforementioned Linklaters.

With the blessings of its auditors and legal consiglieri, Lehman was now resonating at a dangerously unsustainable harmonic frequency. The pendulous energy of the money traveling back and forth across the Atlantic caused a lethal kinetic excitement. It was bound to catch the attention of someone. Lehman Brothers was the only big investment bank that was allowed to fail, and fail it did.

An odd footnote to Lehman's collapse: More than a decade after the fall, collectors are snapping up Lehman-branded merch – unholy relics like Lehman coffee mugs, paperweights, hooded rain ponchos, baby bibs, duffles and flashlights. They are unique because they relate to one of the greatest cautionary tales in American business.

Investment bankers and wealth managers give them as gifts to special clients. They are imbued with the nostalgic fairy dust from an epic tale of greed, hubris and groupthink.

Millennials – some who were in middle school during the crisis – are also snapping up the swag.

"The way people dress today is all about showing off your knowledge, your awareness of cultures and subcultures," Jack Carlson told the Financial Times in 2020. Carlson is the founder of Rowing Blazers, a manufacturer of preppy-chic, vintage-looking clothes.

The Lehman swag tells of a Wall Street bank that bet the farm on a single asset class, refused to cut its losses and expected a government-engineered rescue that never materialized.

"Lehman's story demonstrates that even a massive company can be destroyed be a few people and a couple bad decisions," said the unnamed senior auditor. "It really is that delicate, and I see it often."

February 8, 2007 – August 8, 2007

Gathering Storm

Thursday, February 8, 2007 – HSBC, Europe's largest bank, warns that bad-debt write-downs for 2006 would be 20 percent higher than previously forecast, at about $10.5 billion.

Thursday, February 22, 2007 – HSBC fires the head of its U.S. mortgage-lending business as losses are confirmed at $10.5 billion.

Monday, February 26, 2007 – Former Federal Reserve Chairman Alan Greenspan warns that the economy could fall into recession by the end of 2007, according to a published report. Greenspan tells a business conference that it is difficult to predict the timing of recessions but that it was "possible" that one could occur later in the year, reports the Wall Street Journal.

Tuesday, February 27, 2007 – The U.S. stock market sees its biggest one-day decline since 2003 as reports of a dip in home prices and a steep drop in durable goods orders seem to worry investors. The Dow Jones Industrial Average tumbles 416 points, the biggest point loss since September 17, 2001, the first day of trading after the attacks of September 11. It is the seventh biggest one-day point drop for the Dow. The broader S&P 500 index falls about 3.5 percent – its worst one-day percentage loss since 2003.

Defaults on home loans to so-called "subprime borrowers" – borrowers with poor credit histories – have spiked in recent months, exposing a relaxation of lending standards over the previous two years and forcing more than 20 small subprime lenders to close their doors. Mortgage guarantors Fannie Mae and Freddie Mac announce they have little exposure to the subprime mortgage market.

In addition, Freddie Mac announces it will no longer purchase the most risky subprime loans, known as "2-28 ARMs," adjustable-rate mortgages that reset to a much higher interest rate after the first two years of the 30-year term. The decision is billed as a way the mortgage giant will protect borrowers from predatory lending practices.

From September on, Freddie Mac says it will stop buying "no income, no assets" mortgages, in which borrowers are not asked to provide financial information; "stated income, stated assets" products, for which borrowers' incomes are not easily verifiable; and certain types of mortgages offered with teaser rates.

"The steps we are taking today will provide more protection to consumers and enhance the level of underwriting standards in the market," Freddie Mac's chief executive, Richard Syron, tells the Financial Times.

Wednesday, February 28, 2007 – New-home sales are reported to be down 20.1 percent in January over the same period in 2006. New-home sales are down more than 50 percent year over year in the Western United States, the largest percentage drop in the region since 1981.

U.S. Federal Reserve Chairman Ben Bernanke testifies before the House Budget Committee, telling members of Congress that U.S. financial markets appear to be "working well" and functioning normally, but "the near-term prospects for the housing market remain uncertain," he says. "Sales of new homes have fallen, and continuing declines in starts have not yet led to meaningful reductions in the inventory of homes for sale," he said. "Even if the demand for housing falls no further, weakness in residential construction is likely to remain a drag on economic growth for a time as homebuilders try to reduce their inventories of unsold homes to more normal levels."

Tuesday, March 6, 2007 – The Dow Jones Industrial Average soars 157 points or 1.3 percent after falling more than 600 points from its recent all-time high of 12,786. The broader S&P 500 index ends the day up almost 1.6 percent, while the Nasdaq composite adds 1.9 percent.

Speaking at the Independent Community Bankers of America's Annual Convention and Techworld in Honolulu, U.S. Federal Reserve Chairman Ben Bernanke, quoting Alan Greenspan, warns that the Government Sponsored Enterprises Fannie Mae and Freddie Mac are a source of "systemic risk." He suggests legislation to avert a potential crisis.

Wednesday, March 7, 2007 – DR Horton, the largest U.S. homebuilder by volume, warns of losses from subprime fallout. The company's chief executive, Donald Tomnitz, tells investors the weak U.S. housing market will continue to affect home prices during the year. "I don't want to be too sophisticated here, but '07 is going to suck, all 12 months of the calendar year," he says.

Tuesday, March 13, 2007 – Stocks slump with the Dow Jones Industrial Average losing over 240 points, or 2 percent of its market valuation. The broader S&P 500 index and the Nasdaq composite each fall about 2 percent. It is the second-worst selloff of the year.

Friday, March 16, 2007 – Accredited Home Lenders Holding, a U.S. subprime lender, announces it will sell $2.7 billion of its subprime loans to raise cash to ease recent pressures from margin calls. The loans, it is announced, are sold at a substantial discount. Late mortgage payments are now at a record high.

Monday, April 2, 2007 – New Century Financial, the largest independent nonprime lender in the United States, files for bankruptcy protection as its defaults surge. The Irvine, California-based company, once a high-flier in the risky subprime sector, fires 3,200 employees, or 54 percent of its work force. In its Chapter 11 filing, the lender lists liabilities of more than $100 million. Founded more than a decade earlier by a trio of executives from another subprime lending firm, New Century wrote nearly $51.6 billion in mortgages in 2006 and employed more than 7,200 people.

Separately, it is reported that sales of existing U.S. homes fell 8.4 percent in March, the sharpest month-on-month drop in 18 years and a further sign of weakness in the U.S. housing market. The latest figures show an 11.3 percent decline in existing home sales, compared with the same time a year earlier.

Wednesday, April 11, 2007 – A spate of mortgage delinquencies is not expected to hurt the broader economy, says U.S. Federal Reserve Chairman Ben Bernanke.

"We believe the effect of the troubles in the subprime sector on the broader housing market will likely be limited, and we do not expect significant spillovers from the subprime market to the rest of the economy or to the financial system," said the Fed chairman in remarks to a Chicago Fed conference.

Tuesday, April 17, 2007 – Top executives at U.S. mortgage giants Fannie Mae and Freddie Mac unveil new types of loans to help borrowers with high-risk mortgages avoid losing their homes. Fannie Mae's program will be called "HomeStay," while Freddie Mac's will be called "Home Possible."

Wednesday, April 18, 2007 – Federally chartered mortgage guarantor Freddie Mac is fined $3.8 million by the Federal Election Commission for making illegal campaign contributions, much of them funneled to members of the influential U.S. House Committee on Financial Services, which helps oversee the mortgage guarantor. The agency determined Freddie Mac had violated laws or regulations that prohibit its participation in campaign fund-raising activities.

Wednesday, April 25, 2007 – The Dow Jones Industrial Average closes above 13,000 for the first time in its history.

Thursday, April 26, 2007 – For the first time since 1999, the amount Americans owe on home-equity lines of credit declines, report Equifax and Moody's. Durable goods orders for March for big-ticket items like machinery and electrical equipment rose 3.4 percent to $214.9 billion, reports the U.S.

Commerce Department, allaying worries among investors that capital investment might be slowing.

Wednesday, May 2, 2007 – General Motors' finance arm GMAC reports nearly $1 billion in quarterly losses on its mortgage business, primarily due to subprime mortgage losses.

Thursday, May 3, 2007 – The Zurich-based bank UBS shutters its U.S. subprime lending unit, Dillon Read Capital Management. The move brings to an end the bank's high-profile effort to run an in-house Wall Street hedge fund after suffering big losses betting on America's subprime mortgage industry.

Monday, May 21, 2007 – The National Association of Business Economists downgrades its forecast for economic growth for 2007 from 2.8 percent to 2.3 percent.

Wednesday, May 30, 2007 – U.K. subprime lender Kensington accepts a takeover offer from the South African bank Investec.

Thursday, June 7, 2007 – Bear Stearns halts redemptions in two of its collateralized debt-obligation hedge funds: the High-Grade Structured Credit Strategies Enhanced Leverage Fund and the High-Grade Structured Credit Fund.

Saturday, June 9, 2007 – Former U.S. Federal Reserve governor Edward Gramlich tells the Wall Street Journal that former Fed Chairman Alan Greenspan had, when in office, blocked a proposal to increase scrutiny of subprime lenders under the Fed's broad authority.

Tuesday, June 19, 2007 – The National Association of Realtors predicts a one percent decline nationwide in existing home prices for 2007, the first such prediction in the nearly half-century the industry association has tracked home prices. It also foresees home sales will decline 4.6 percent to 6.18 million in 2007, compared with its previous forecast of a 2.9 percent decline. In 2006, 6.48 million homes were sold. The organization predicts an even sharper drop of 18.2 percent in new home sales.

Wednesday, June 20, 2007 – Merrill Lynch seizes about $800 million in assets from ailing hedge funds managed by Bear Stearns, casting doubt on the funds' survival.

Separately, Bear Stearns reveals it will spend $3.2 billion bailing out a troubled hedge fund exposed to the subprime market.

Tuesday, July 10, 2007 – Standard and Poor's Rating Services abruptly announces it is putting 612 securities backed by subprime mortgages on "CreditWatch negative" and that it expects most to soon be downgraded because of high delinquency and foreclosure rates. Moody's Investors Service drops a similar bombshell. It announces it will be downgrading 399 securities and will be placing an additional 32 securities on review for possible downgrade, reports the news service Reuters. Just two days later, rival Fitch Ratings will announce it has placed 170 U.S. subprime transactions among its $428 billion universe of rated subprime transactions as "Under Analysis," indicating that Fitch will be issuing a rating action over the coming several weeks. Many of the loans are in the portfolios of Wall Street players like Bear Stearns, Citigroup, JPMorgan, Merrill Lynch and Morgan Stanley.

Friday, July 13, 2007 – General Electric announces it will abandon the subprime mortgage market by selling WMC Mortgage, the company's unit that makes loans to borrowers with weak credit histories. "The mortgage industry has greatly changed since the purchase of WMC," said its chief executive, Laurent Bossard.

Thursday, July 19, 2007 – For the first time in its history, the Dow Jones Industrial Average closes above 14,000.

U.S. Federal Reserve chairman Ben Bernanke warns that the crisis in the U.S. subprime lending market could cost up to $100 billion and threaten consumer spending.

Friday, July 27, 2007 – The Dow industrials plummet for the second straight session, with the 30-stock index falling more than 200 points, marking the index's worst week in over 4 years.

Tuesday, July 31, 2007 – Global investment bank Bear Stearns announces it has halted redemptions in a hedge fund that invested in securities backed by subprime mortgage loans after panicky investors sought to pull out their money. This follows the liquidation of two failed hedge funds.

Friday, August 3, 2007 – The Dow Jones Industrial Average plunges 280 points, or 2.1 percent. The broader S&P 500 loses about 2.7 percent, while the tech-heavy Nasdaq Composite index tumbles 2.5 percent.

CNBC television personality Jim Cramer blasts the chairman of the U.S. Federal Reserve, Ben Bernanke, and other central bankers for their lack of knowledge about the risk the subprime market poses to the financial system. Cramer also criticizes Bill Poole, who at the time is president of the St. Louis Fed. "They know nothing!" he inveighs.

Monday, August 6, 2007 – American Home Mortgage Investment, which specializes in adjustable-rate mortgages, files for bankruptcy protection. The filing comes after American Home, one of the largest U.S. independent home-loan providers, shut down most operations the previous week, laying off all but about 750 workers. The company said it had started the year with more than 7,400 employees.

August 9, 2007 – September 13, 2008

The Dominoes Fall

Thursday, August 9, 2007 – BNP Paribas, France's largest publicly traded bank and the eurozone's second-largest bank by value, announces it is barring investors from redeeming $2.2 billion in three mutual funds, citing the U.S. subprime mortgage sector woes that have rattled financial markets.

"The complete evaporation of liquidity in certain market segments of the U.S. securitization market has made it impossible to value certain assets fairly, regardless of their quality or credit rating," the French bank said in a statement.

The bank identifies the funds as Parvest Dynamic ABS, BNP Paribas ABS Euribor and BNP Paribas ABS Eonia. It marks the beginning of the worst financial crisis since the 1930s.

Separately, German bank Sal. Oppenheim announces it has temporarily frozen a 750 million euro asset-backed securities fund it managed for Austrian investment foundation Hypo KAG, and the Dutch merchant bank NIBC shelved an initial public offering after revealing a 137 million euro loss in losses on U.S. asset-backed securities.

Friday, August 10, 2007 – Central banks, including the U.S. Federal Reserve, the European Central Bank, the Bank of Japan, coordinate to increase liquidity for the first time since the aftermath of the September 11, 2001 terrorist attacks.

The U.K.'s FTSE 100 stock index is battered, closing 3.7 percent lower.

Thursday, August 16, 2007 – Countrywide Financial Corporation, the largest U.S. mortgage lender, taps its entire $11.5 billion bank credit line to offset a liquidity crunch. The company announces it is toughening underwriting standards on home loans. All three major U.S. credit rating agencies downgrade Countrywide debt; at least two analysts have raised the specter of a Countrywide bankruptcy. Fitch Ratings cuts the credit rating to its third-lowest investment-grade rating.

Friday, August 17, 2007 – In a move to soothe spooked financial markets, the U.S. Federal Reserve cuts its discount rate by half a percentage point, to 5.75 percent. The discount rate is the rate the Fed charges lenders, primarily banks, for temporary loans. The Fed does not alter the federal funds rate, which is more closely watched as it affects credit cards, home equity lines of credit, car loans and other consumer loan rates. That rate remains at 5.25 percent.

Monday, August 20, 2007 – After exhausting an $11.5 billion line of credit a week earlier, California-based mortgage lender Countrywide Financial Corporation begins laying off employees in an effort to cut costs.

Tuesday, August 21, 2007 – Capital One Financial Corporation announces it will stop making residential mortgages and close its wholesale mortgage banking unit

GreenPoint Mortgage.

Separately, RealtyTrac, the online marketer of foreclosure properties, reports a 9 percent rise in U.S. foreclosure filings in July over the previous month and a 93 percent jump compared with July 2006.

Thursday, August 23, 2007 – Subprime lender Countrywide receives a $2 billion cash injection from Bank of America. Share prices fall after Countrywide warns that the mortgage slump is getting worse.

Tuesday, August 28, 2007 – The German public-sector regional bank SachsenLB is quickly taken over by Germany's largest regional bank, Landesbank Baden-Wuerttemberg. News of Leipzig-based SachsenLB's woes came a week earlier when it said it received a $23.7 billion credit line from other banks, to help it overcome risk from the subprime exposure of an Irish-based unit.

Thursday, August 30, 2007 – German Chancellor Angela Merkel criticizes the credit-rating agencies for not identifying problems in the market.

Friday, August 31, 2007 – Ameriquest Mortgage Company, once the largest subprime lender in the United States, closes after Citigroup announces it has agreed to acquire the wholesale origination and mortgage-servicing business of Ameriquest's parent, ACC Capital Holdings, for an undisclosed price. Founded in 1979, Orange, California-based Ameriquest — "sponsor of the American dream" — began as Long Beach Savings & Loan, a California-based thrift.

U.S. President George W. Bush announces a limited bailout of U.S. homeowners unable to afford the mounting costs of their mortgages but warns that the federal government will not bail out real estate speculators.

Monday, September 3, 2007 – German lender IKB Industriebank cautions investors that it expects to lose almost $1 billion as a result of exposure to U.S. subprime mortgages.

Tuesday, September 4, 2007 – In a sign that banks are reluctant to lend to one another, the 3-month London Interbank Offered Rate, or Libor, reaches 6.7975 percent, exceeding the Bank of England's emergency lending rate to banks of 5.75 percent. The last time the Libor had reached these heights was after the collapse of U.S. hedge fund Long Term Capital Management.

Thursday, September 6, 2007 – The European Central Bank injects $57 billion into banks to boost liquidity after warning of fresh volatility in financial markets. The U.S. Federal Reserve makes $31.25 billion in temporary loans to U.S. money markets.

Friday, September 14, 2007 – Britain's Northern Rock bank seeks and receives standby funding from the Bank of England, citing "extreme conditions." Lines begin to form outside a number of Northern Rock branches as spooked depositors seek to withdraw their money in person and online. Northern Rock becomes the first British bank to experience a bank run in more than 140 years, losing more than $25 billion to withdrawals in September, two-thirds of which are taken out via online withdrawals, telephone transactions and wire transfers in a so-called "silent bank run." The bank's website crashes under the strain, reports the BBC, and all its phone lines are jammed. The emergency funding will enable the bank to "fund its operations during the current period of turbulence in financial markets." Northern Rock chief executive Adam Applegarth emphasizes it is "business as usual" for the institution, but his comments do not allay the fears of analysts or depositors. The bank's shares plummet 32 percent over worries about its viability.

Tuesday, September 18, 2007 – The U.S. Federal Reserve lowers the benchmark federal funds rate by 75 basis points to 4.75 percent in an acknowledgment of potential damage to the economy from the housing and credit crises.

Thursday, September 20, 2007 – Investment bank Goldman Sachs sees its earnings soar 79 percent – far above expectations. It is helped by betting correctly that the value of mortgage bonds would plunge. While the firm's losses caused by the subprime crisis were $1.5 billion, it reports this was "more than offset" by its hedging that mortgage bonds would tumble. Its earnings for the quarter rises to $2.85 billion from $1.58 billion a year earlier.

Friday, September 28, 2007 – CNBC's Jim Cramer warns Americans on "The Today Show," "Don't you dare buy a home now — you will lose money." Charles McMillan, president-elect of the National Association of Realtors, tells television host Matt Lauer, "It is a wonderful time [to buy a home] and it's a wonderful idea." He recommends "buying in markets in Indiana, Michigan, Ohio or some of those areas."

Internet banking pioneer NetBank, an online bank with $2.5 billion in assets, is shut down by U.S. federal regulators.

Monday, October 1, 2007 – Swiss bank UBS, the world's largest wealth manager, discloses losses of $3.4 billion in its fixed income and rates division, and in its mortgage-backed securities business. The bank says it plans to slash 1,500 jobs and make sweeping management changes. It is one of the biggest casualties yet from the global credit crisis.

Meanwhile, Citigroup announces that deterioration in the mortgage-backed securities and credit markets are expected to have an adverse impact on its third-quarter financial results.

Friday, October 5, 2007 – Investment bank Merrill Lynch warns it will report a third-quarter loss, with its bottom line taking a $4.5 billion hit for bad investments linked to defaulted U.S. subprime mortgages.

Tuesday, October 9, 2007 – Stocks rally, sending the Dow Jones Industrial Average and the broader S&P 500 indices to all-time highs. The Dow Jones Industrial Average closes at its peak at 14,164.53. This high will not be revisited until March 5, 2013, when a new peak is set.

Monday, October 15, 2007 – Citigroup writes down an additional $5.9 billion due to exposure to the U.S. subprime market, reporting that third-quarter profits dropped 57 percent after its fixed-income and consumer businesses were pummeled. The news helps send the stock market into a sharp decline.

Separately, Nomura Holdings, the largest Japanese brokerage, announces it will close its U.S. mortgage-backed securities business and take a $621 million hit in its first quarterly pretax loss in four years.

Monday, October 17, 2007 – Housing construction in the United States fell by 10.2 percent in September, the U.S.

Commerce Department reports. It is worse than analysts have predicted. Applications for building permits, considered a bellwether for future activity, also fell sharply in September, dropping by 7.3 percent.

Tuesday, October 30, 2007 – Merrill Lynch takes a $7.9 billion write-down following exposure to bad debt. At this time, it is the largest such loss taken by any Wall Street firm and $3.4 billion more than Merrill had predicted just three weeks earlier. Merrill's chief executive, Stan O'Neal, resigns after a boardroom drama.

Wednesday, October 31, 2007 – The Federal Open Market Committee votes to lower its target for the Federal funds rate 25 basis points to 4.5 percent, citing continued concerns about weakness in the housing market. But the vote was not unanimous, reflecting disagreement among policymakers about the risks that await the economy.

Separately, Deutsche Bank announces a $3 billion write-down on bad debts.

Sunday, November 4, 2007 – Citigroup announces it will post a new round of write-downs of as much as $11 billion due to exposure to the U.S. subprime market. Citi's chief executive and chairman, Charles Prince, resigns. Shares of Citigroup stock fall nearly 5 percent in trading.

Wednesday, November 7, 2007 – Morgan Stanley confirms it will take a $3.7 billion fourth-quarter write-down as a result of its subprime mortgage exposure.

After temporarily freezing $2.1 billion in hedge-fund assets in August, BNP Paribas reveals it has written down $439 million due to credit problems, including $197 million related to U.S. subprime mortgages and homebuilder lending.

Friday, November 9, 2007 – Wachovia, the fourth-largest lender in the United States, announces it will absorb a $1.1 billion loss due to a decline in value of its mortgage debt, plus $600 million to cover loan losses.

Monday, November 12, 2007 – The three biggest U.S. banks – Citigroup, Bank of America and JPMorgan Chase – agree to simplify a $75 billion superfund to purchase bad debt in an effort to restore confidence in credit markets.

Tuesday, November 13, 2007 – Bank of America, the second-largest bank in the United States, announces it will take a $3 billion write-down due to subprime losses.

Wednesday, November 14, 2007 – Three of Japan's biggest banks – Mizuho Financial Group, Shinsei Bank and Aozora Bank – unveil steep declines in first-half results and cut their full-year profit forecasts due to losses related to subprime mortgages.

Thursday, November 15, 2007 – The U.S. House of Representatives passes the Predatory Lending and Mortgage Protection Act. It would regulate mortgage brokers and loan officers, requiring them to be licensed. It would also require lenders to take steps to ensure prospective borrowers are able to repay their loans.

The British bank Barclays confirms it has exposure to U.S. home loans; it will write down $2.7 billion in subprime losses.

The Financial Accounting Standards Board implements a new accounting regulation known as the "mark-to-market" accounting rule. It involves determining the value of an asset to reflect current market conditions. It becomes a ticking time bomb.

Friday, November 16, 2007 – Adam Applegarth, the chief executive of the ailing British bank Northern Rock, will leave his position by the end of January, the bank confirms. The bank's shares collapsed after it was forced to seek emergency funding from the Bank of England in September. Spooked depositors rushed to withdraw their money; the bank has since been seeking bidders to rescue it.

Wall Street bank Goldman Sachs' chief economist, Jan Hatzius, forecasts losses from cratered credit markets will reduce lending by $2 trillion, and losses for financial companies related to record U.S. home foreclosures will be as high as $400 billion.

Monday, November 19, 2007 – The 144-year-old Swiss Re, the world's largest reinsurance company, announces it expects to lose about $1 billion on insurance payouts to a client – believed to be a bank. The client had purchased a policy against any fall in the value of its mortgage debt. Swiss Re did not provide the name of the client.

In a conference call with analysts, Roger W. Ferguson, Jr., head of the company's financial services division, acknowledged that the company "clearly made some poor choices."

The news intensifies the perception of risk in the insurance industry, William Hawkins, an analyst at Keefe, Bruyette & Woods, tells the New York Times. "At a time when we thought the risk management of the insurance sector was getting better," he said, "today's announcement is a serious blow to confidence."

Tuesday, November 20, 2007 – U.S. mortgage guarantor Freddie Mac reports a $2 billion loss and sets aside $1.2 billion to cover bad loans.

Wednesday, November 21, 2007 – Asset manager BlackRock is tapped to manage a $75 billion fund put together by U.S. banks at the behest of Treasury Secretary Henry Paulson, reports the Financial Times, citing unnamed sources. The trio of banks – Citigroup, JPMorgan Chase and Bank of America – are reported to have set up the superfund, designed to provide liquidity to struggling structured investment vehicles that bought asset-backed commercial paper and mortgage-backed securities that lost value.

Tuesday, November 27, 2007 – U.S. mortgage guarantor Freddie Mac announces it will sell $6 billion of preferred shares "in light of actual and anticipated losses."

Citigroup, the largest U.S. bank, agrees to a cash infusion of $7.5 billion by an investment fund owned by Abu Dhabi, signaling the growing clout of sovereign wealth funds.

Most large U.S. lenders have now reported exposure to subprime mortgage debt.

Home prices in the United States dropped sharply in the third quarter, the steepest fall in 21 years, a survey shows.

Wednesday, November 28, 2007 – The Norwegian brokerage Terra Securities ASA declares bankruptcy after national regulators move to revoke its license for failing to inform four Norwegian townships of the high risk of their U.S. investments. The townships had been embroiled in a dispute with Terra over losses, asserting the investment house failed to inform them of the high risk of 451 million kroner ($82 million) in investments placed through Citibank.

The townships of Rana, Hemnes, Hattfjelldal and Narvik – all in northern Norway – rejected a settlement offer from Terra Securities, saying it would effectively mean losing their entire investment. After declaring bankruptcy, Terra said there would be no money to offer the townships. In 2001, the four townships borrowed money to invest in the complicated bonds. The municipalities had also signed a confidentiality clause with Terra, which ensured that no independent third party could evaluate the quality of the investments.

Thursday, November 29, 2007 – Morgan Stanley co-president Zoe Cruz, a 25-year veteran of the firm and one of the most influential women on Wall Street, announces she will retire, becoming the latest casualty in the unfolding U.S. subprime crisis.

Friday, November 30, 2007 – U.S. residential construction spending declines, led by a steep fall in home construction.

Tuesday, December 4, 2007 – U.S. mortgage guarantor Fannie Mae announces it will issue $7 billion of preferred stock to cover losses linked to the housing market. The government-sponsored mortgage giant will cut its dividend 30 percent.

The Bank of Canada announces it will cut its key overnight interest rate by a quarter of a percentage point to 4.25 percent for the first time since April 2004 amid credit fears.

Thursday, December 6, 2007 – The U.S. government throws a lifeline to homeowners affected by the U.S. housing slump. The White House says the plan, which will streamline the mortgage modification process, could help as many as 1.2

million distressed homeowners. The plan includes a five-year freeze on interest rates for borrowers current with their monthly payments.

Royal Bank of Scotland Group says it anticipates write-downs of nearly $2.6 billion due to U.S. subprime lending losses.

The Bank of England cuts its benchmark interest rate by a quarter-point to 5.5 percent. It is the British central bank's first reduction of rates since 2005. The bank said the trans-Atlantic credit crunch had curtailed loans for households and businesses, denting Britain's growth prospects.

Monday, December 10, 2007 – The Swiss bank UBS reveals a further $10 billion in write-downs caused by bad debt in the U.S. housing market, making it the biggest victim of the U.S. subprime crisis among major European banks. Singapore, it is also announced, will take 9 percent of UBS in a deal that mirrors actions resorted to by U.S.-based Citigroup.

Tuesday, December 11, 2007 – The U.S. Federal Reserve cuts short-term interest rates by a quarter of a point to 4.25 percent to ease the worsening mortgage fallout.

Thursday, December 13, 2007 – The central banks of five nations, including the U.S. Federal Reserve and the Bank of England, agree to coordinate their actions to inject at least $100 billion into short-term interbank credit markets to restore confidence.

Citigroup announces it will put $49 billion of subprime debt back on its balance sheet, effectively assuming the losses from seven so-called "structured investment vehicles." Moody's Investors Service cuts the bank's debt ratings.

Friday, December 14, 2007 – Moody's reaffirms its triple-A rating of bond insurers MBIA and Ambac Financial Group.

Sunday, December 16, 2007 – Former Fed chairman Alan Greenspan calls on the U.S. government to provide direct assistance to homeowners hit by the subprime crisis.

Monday, December 17, 2007 – The U.S. Federal Reserve makes $20 billion available, at auction, to commercial banks. The goal is to encourage the banks to borrow from the Fed and, in so doing, boost lending to businesses and consumers.

Wall Street extends the previous week's losses. The Dow Jones Industrial Average falls nearly 175 points, and all the major indices lose at least 1 percent.

Tuesday, December 18, 2007 – The U.S. Federal Reserve tightens its rules on subprime lending, requiring mortgage lenders to provide greater scrutiny of borrower income and full disclosure of the cost of the loan.

The European Central Bank begins pumping a record $500 billion into European commercial banks to help ease the credit crisis. Similarly, the Bank of England conducts auctions, like those undertaken by the Federal Reserve, to make funds available to U.K. banks.

Wednesday, December 19, 2007 – Morgan Stanley takes an additional $5.7 billion write-down due to subprime losses and announces it will accept a $5 billion cash infusion from a Chinese state investment company in order to recapitalize. The investment bank also announces fourth-quarter losses of $3.6 billion, or $3.61 a share. It represents the first quarterly loss in Morgan Stanley's 72-year history. John Mack, its chairman and chief executive, calls the news "embarrassing."

Standard & Poor's downgrades the credit ratings of monoline bond insurers ACA Financial Guaranty, Ambac Assurance Corp.; MBIA Insurance Corp.; XL Capital Assurance Inc.; and Financial Guaranty Insurance Co.

Friday, December 21, 2007 – A consortium of three major U.S. banks abandons the U.S. government-supported "super-SIV" mortgage crisis bailout plan announced in mid-October, citing a lack of demand for the risky mortgage products on which the plan was based.

Friday, January 4, 2008 – The U.S. unemployment report for December 2007 shows a sharp rise in joblessness as the unemployment rate shot up to 5 percent, a two-year high. The report by the U.S. Bureau of Labor Statistics sparks a fall in stock market. Stocks tumble, with the Dow Jones Industrial Average shedding over 250 points.

Wednesday, January 9, 2008 – Bear Stearns' longtime chief executive James "Jimmy" Cayne joins the exodus of Wall Street CEOs as the investment bank announces $1.9 billion in subprime losses, the largest in the bank's history.

Thursday, January 10, 2008 – The U.S. city of Cleveland, Ohio, files a lawsuit against 21 major financial institutions, alleging their activities in connection with securitization of subprime mortgages created a "public nuisance," violating state law.

Friday, January 11, 2008 – Countrywide Financial Corporation, the largest mortgage lender in the United States, is acquired by Bank of America. Calabasas, California-based Countrywide, a pioneer of subprime mortgage lending, was bleeding cash as a growing number of borrowers were defaulting on their mortgages. As the deal is announced, Bank of America is experiencing a growth spurt, due mostly to acquisitions. The bank is eager to expand its mortgage business. Bank of America will later end up losing over $40 billion on the deal and be embroiled in legal matters for years over the acquisition.

Tuesday, January 15, 2008 – Citigroup reports a $9.8 billion loss for the fourth quarter, announcing it will write down $18 billion in subprime losses. Citi, the largest bank in the United States, also announces that stakes will be taken in the group by Kuwaiti and Saudi Arabian sovereign wealth funds.

Wednesday, January 16, 2008 – The U.S. bank JPMorgan Chase reveals that its fourth-quarter earnings declined by 34 percent, attributing the loss to a $1.3 billion hit related to its holdings of bad subprime mortgage loans.

Thursday, January 17, 2008 – Merrill Lynch, the world's largest brokerage, announces its worst quarterly loss ever, as it absorbs a $14.6 billion hit from losses driven primarily by a $11.5 billion write-down the company took on its subprime residential mortgages and collateralized debt obligations.

The investment bank Lehman Brothers cuts 1,300 jobs as it pares back its U.S. mortgage lending operations. With the cuts, Lehman will have eliminated 3,750 mortgage jobs worldwide since June 2007.

Monday, January 21, 2008 – The London FTSE stock index falls 5.5 percent, its largest one-day loss since September 11, 2001. Stocks fleetingly rebound. Investors react with what analysts describe as panic over the weakening U.S. economy.

Tuesday, January 22, 2008 – The U.S. Federal Reserve cuts the benchmark federal funds rate by 75 basis points to 3.5 percent. It is the biggest cut in 25 years.

With auto-loan default rates quickly rising, AmeriCredit doubles its provision for loan losses.

Thursday, January 24, 2008 – The National Association of Realtors announces that in 2007, the median price of a single-family home in the United States declined for the first time in at least four decades. The median home price, according to the trade group, fell 1.8 percent to $217,800, the first annual decline since reliable records began in 1968. "It's the first price decline in many, many years and possibly going back to the Great Depression," said the group's chief economist, Lawrence Yun.

Monday, January 28, 2008 – The Belgian bank Fortis warns of losses due to bad U.S. mortgage debt that could be as high as $1.5 billion.

Tuesday, January 29, 2008 – The U.S. Federal Bureau of Investigation announces it has launched a probe into 14 companies involved in the subprime mortgage crisis.

Wednesday, January 30, 2008 – The U.S. Federal Reserve cuts the benchmark federal funds rate by 50 basis points, to 3 percent.

UBS, the largest Swiss bank, announces it will write off $14 billion in losses stemming from the U.S. housing market.

Thursday, January 31, 2008 – Bond insurer MBIA announces a $2.3 billion quarterly loss. It cites write-downs the company took on its insured credit derivatives portfolio.

Friday, February 1, 2008 – In the latest allegation that title-insurance companies colluded illegally and paid kickbacks to brokers to secure new business, an antitrust lawsuit is filed in federal court in New York against the four firms that dominate title insurance nationwide. The lawsuit alleges consumers across the State of New York paid hundreds of millions of dollars in extra closing costs due to price-fixing. The lawsuit names four big firms that control nearly 90 percent of the market: Fidelity National Title Group, First American Corporation, LandAmerica Financial Group and Stewart Title Insurance.

Tuesday, February 5, 2008 – The U.S. consumer finance firm GMAC, which owns subprime lender Residential Capital, reports a $2.3 billion loss for 2007.

Thursday, February 7, 2008 – The chairman of the U.S. Federal Reserve, Ben Bernanke, says he believes the fallout affecting bond insurers could have a detrimental effect on financial markets. Analysts fear the insurers will not be able to make good on claims, forcing banks to announce another big round of losses.

The market for auction-rate securities seizes up when lead underwriters choose not to support the auctions. This leaves investors with illiquid assets.

Deutsche Bank, which took $3.2 billion of subprime write-downs in the third quarter of 2007, reports it did not suffer subprime-related losses in the fourth quarter. Compared with write-downs taken by Citigroup, Merrill Lynch and UBS, Germany's largest bank appears to have dodged the worst of the subprime mortgage crisis.

The Bank of England's Monetary Policy Committee votes to reduce the official bank rate paid on commercial bank reserves by 25 basis points to 5.25 percent.

Sunday, February 10, 2008 – After a meeting of the Group of Seven industrialized nations in Tokyo, Peer Steinbrück, German finance minister, says the G7 is worried that worldwide write-offs on U.S. subprime mortgages could reach $400 billion. In a joint statement, the leaders assert economic fundamentals remained "solid" but that downside risks remain. "We will continue to take appropriate actions, individually and collectively, in order to secure stability and growth in our economies."

Tuesday, February 12, 2008 – Zurich-based Credit Suisse reports losses on subprime investments at $1.8 billion, less than analysts had forecast. By contrast, its crosstown rival, UBS, reported in January that it had written down $14 billion for the same period.

American International Group will be forced to write down the value of financial instruments tied to mortgages after its auditors, PricewaterhouseCoopers, takes a hard line, saying it found "material weakness" in its accounting system and how it valued credit-default swaps. AIG shares hit a 5-year low in trading.

Berkshire Hathaway Chairman Warren Buffett offers to reinsure $800 billion in municipal bonds already guaranteed by embattled bond insurers Ambac Financial Group, MBIA and Financial Guaranty Insurance Co.. He would reinsure municipal bonds for which the companies had already written policies but charge 1.5 times the remaining premiums the insurers would earn on existing policies.

Wednesday, February 13, 2008 – U.S. President George W. Bush signs the Economic Stimulus Act of 2008. The measure aims to fend off a recession by stimulating consumer and business spending. It provides a rebate to individuals who file a tax return for 2007 or 2008, effectively lowering their federal tax rate. It temporarily increases certain business tax write-offs from $125,000 to $250,000 for purchases of depreciable assets, and up to 50 percent of the cost of certain purchases in 2008. In an attempt to ease the subprime mortgage crisis, the law permits the Federal Housing Authority, Freddie Mac and Fannie Mae to buy up larger mortgages from lenders in certain high-cost areas in the United States.

Japan's financial watchdog, the Financial Services Agency, says Japanese banks suffered losses of $5.6 billion at the close of 2007. The losses are small compared with the hits taken by U.S. and European banks.

Swiss investment bank UBS stuns markets, confirming a loss of $4 billion in 2007 after writing down the value of investments in U.S. mortgages, leveraged finance and complex securities by $18.4 billion. The annual loss is the first since UBS was created in 1998 from the merger of Union Bank of Switzerland and Swiss Bank Corporation.

Thursday, February 14, 2008 – New York Governor Eliot Spitzer, testifying before members of the U.S. Congress, says bond insurers have a 3- to 5-day window to recapitalize or find other solutions to their problems. The once obscure bond insurers have come to the forefront in the financial crisis. They now risk their triple-A credit ratings.

Commerzbank, Germany's second-largest publicly traded bank, writes down $1.1 billion from the value of investments linked to U.S. subprime mortgages and announces its fourth-quarter profits fell by 44 percent.

Citigroup suspends redemptions on one of its hedge funds, known as CSO Partners. The move comes after investors try to withdraw about 30 percent of the fund's $500 million in assets.

Another obscure corner of the insurance industry, mortgage insurance, is put into sharp relief as it sees an increase in claims on policies sold by companies like MGIC Investment Corporation, Radian Group, PMI Group and Triad Guaranty threaten credit-rating downgrades.

Moody's Investors Service cuts its triple-A rating for bond insurer FGIC Corp., reducing it to A3.

Sunday, February 17, 2008 – Britain's Northern Rock bank is nationalized, opening a new chapter in the unfolding crisis. It is a temporary measure, announces the U.K.'s Chancellor of the Exchequer, Alistair Darling. This comes after two private proposals to take over the embattled bank fail to offer "sufficient value for money to the taxpayer," says Darling, who adds the public will gain if the government holds on to Northern Rock until market conditions improve.

Tuesday, February 19, 2008 – The 111-year-old Dow Jones Industrial Average adds Bank of America and Chevron Corporation to its 30-component stocks, removing Honeywell International and cigarette maker Altria Group.

Many small banks that simply steered clear of bets on risky mortgages have outperformed the equity markets, being 6 percent or less below their 52-week highs. "The formula is so simple a kid could do it," Ron Hermance, CEO of Paramus, New Jersey-based Hudson City Bancorp, told USA Today. His bank reported a 9 percent higher fourth-quarter profit and saw its stock increase 4 percent in the new year. The bank's growth led to its inclusion in the S&P 500 index in 2007. Hermance would be the recipient of many awards, including Mad Money's "George Bailey Banker of the Year" from Jim Cramer in 2008, and Best Managed Bank of 2007 by Forbes Magazine.

Wednesday, March 5, 2008 – France's biggest retail bank, Credit Agricole, posts a fourth-quarter loss, hit by a $5 billion write-down at its Calyon investment banking arm due to U.S. subprime mortgage losses.

Thursday, March 6, 2008 – Failing to meet margin calls, a fund run by Peloton Partners collapses. The fund is linked to the private equity firm Carlyle Group.

Friday, March 7, 2008 – The former bosses of Merrill Lynch, Countrywide and Citigroup are questioned by the House Committee on Government and Oversight Reform over their pay and bonuses in light of enormous subprime-related losses at their banks. Between 2002 and the close of 2006, the trio were paid a combined $460 million, according to a report issued by the Congressional committee.

Monday, March 10, 2008 – The Dow Jones Industrial Average slumps to its lowest level since October 2006, falling more than 20 percent from its peak just five months earlier.

Tuesday, March 11, 2008 – The Fed invokes emergency powers to lend up to $200 billion in Treasury notes to so-called "primary dealers," a group of 20 big investment firms that broker bond sales. The primary dealers have been saddled with mortgage-backed securities and other collateralized debt obligations they haven't been able to resell on the secondary market. Many investors are now avoiding these mortgage-backed securities, fearing defaults in the underlying home mortgages will erode their value.

Wednesday, March 12, 2008 – Investment bank Bear Stearns maintains all is well. Via a live feed from The Breakers resort in Palm Beach, Bear's chief executive Alan Schwartz tells CNBC, "We don't see any pressure on our liquidity, let alone a liquidity crisis."

Friday, March 14, 2008 – Bear Stearns gets a $25 billion lifeline from the U.S. Federal Reserve. The initial announcement does not indicate how much funding Bear Stearns will receive. With the money, the firm will "have the ability to fund ourselves every day, to do business as usual. It's a bridge to a more permanent solution," says chief executive Alan Schwartz, who tells CNN Money the firm's liquidity crunch hit the previous day, as many customers demanded cash after hearing rumors of trouble. Schwartz says the firm's capital position is in "good shape."

Separately, the private equity giant Carlyle Group has pledged to "stand by" its investors in the firm's failed billion dollar hedge fund, the Financial Times reports. Carlyle Capital invested in securities issued by Fannie Mae and Freddie Mac.

Sunday, March 16, 2008 – Bear Stearns, America's fifth-largest investment bank, collapses and is sold to JPMorgan Chase for $2 a share – a 93 percent discount off Bear's last closing stock price. The U.S. government-engineered transaction is backed by financing from the U.S. Federal Reserve and the U.S. Treasury. The takeover underscores the risks banks and financial companies face as the U.S. mortgage crisis worsens. The $2-per-share price raises fears over banking-sector valuation.

"The fact that the Bear Stearns board is letting these assets go at such a deep discount brings into question the value of assets on a lot of corporate balance sheets," Timothy

Ghriskey, chief investment officer at Solaris Asset Management in New York, tells CNBC.

Tuesday, March 18, 2008 – The U.S. Federal Reserve lowers the federal funds rate by 75 basis points to 2.25 percent, citing recent information indicating the outlook for economic activity has weakened further.

Tuesday, March 25, 2008 – U.S. Senator and presidential hopeful John McCain cautions against premature government action to remedy the mortgage crisis, saying "it is not the duty of government to bail out and reward those who act irresponsibly, whether they are big banks or small borrowers."

Tuesday, April 1, 2008 – Deutsche Bank Chief Executive Josef Ackermann announces the bank will write down nearly $4 billion in the first quarter on bad loan debt.

Zurich-based UBS, Switzerland's largest bank, unveils a further $19 billion in write-downs due to the U.S. real estate market. This came on top of the $18.4 billion, which it announced for 2007. Marcel Ospel, its chairman, resigns.

Thursday, April 17, 2008 – U.S. investment bank Merrill Lynch announces an additional $4.5 billion in mortgage-related write-downs and a net loss of nearly $2 billion for the first quarter.

Friday, April 18, 2008 – Citigroup, the largest U.S. bank, posts a $5.1 billion loss and unveils more than $15 billion in subprime-related write-downs. The New York-based bank also cuts 9,000 jobs amid a quarterly loss of $5 billion.

Jerry Bowyer, chief economist for Benchmark Financial Network, writes in a New York Sun op-ed that the fault for the subprime crisis "lies with the small army of hard-left political hustlers who spent the early 1990s pushing risky mortgages on home lenders. And the fault lies especially with the legislators that gave them the power to do it."

Tuesday, April 22, 2008 – The United Kingdom's second-largest bank, Royal Bank of Scotland, reveals $12 billion in write-downs, and urges its shareholders to support a record $24 billion cash call to rebuild its cratered balance sheet.

Tuesday, April 29, 2008 – Foreclosure filings are reported up 112 percent from the first quarter of 2007. One of every 194 U.S. households receives a foreclosure filing during the quarter, reports the real estate information firm RealtyTrac.

Tuesday, May 6, 2008 – Zurich-based UBS, the European bank hit hardest by the credit crunch thus far, announces plans to sell $15 billion of subprime mortgage debt and cut 5,500 jobs.

Monday, May 12, 2008 – HSBC, Europe's largest bank, announces a write-down of $3.2 billion for the first quarter of 2008 due to exposure to the U.S. subprime market. It also announces a further $2.6 billion in write-downs in its global banking arm. HSBC now trails Citibank, UBS and Merrill Lynch in its write-downs of bad debt.

Thursday, May 15, 2008 – Barclays announces it has taken a further write-down on assets and announces profits for the first quarter of 2008 will go lower. It confirms its capital ratios will likely decline further but declines to speculate as to how it will boost its capital strength. Barclays does not ask shareholders for additional cash to shore up its balance sheet as Royal Bank of Scotland, HBOS and Bradford & Bingley have now done.

Wednesday, June 18, 2008 – U.S. Senator Christopher Dodd of Connecticut, chairman of the Senate Banking Committee, brings a housing bailout bill to the Senate floor that will assist ailing subprime mortgage lenders like California-based Countrywide Financial. The day before, Dodd admits knowing that Countrywide regarded him as a "special" customer and a "Friend of Angelo," referring to Countrywide CEO Angelo Mozilo. Dodd continues to insist he didn't know he was getting a $75,000 reduction in payments on his personal mortgage through Countrywide.

Thursday, June 19, 2008 – More than 400 real estate and mortgage industry participants have been indicted in the United States since March, including dozens over the prior two days, in a U.S. Justice Department crackdown on mortgage fraud.

Thursday, June 26, 2008 – U.S. Senator Charles Schumer of New York, a member of the Senate Banking Committee, makes public a letter to regulators questioning the solvency of IndyMac Bank. Over the next 11 days, jittery depositors will withdraw a total of $1.3 billion. The director of the Office of Thrift Supervision, John Reich, will fault the senator for causing a run on deposits, ensuring the bank's failure.

Friday, July 11, 2008 – IndyMac Bank is seized by Federal regulators, making it the largest regulated thrift to fail. Operations of the Pasadena, California-based bank, one of the nation's largest home lenders, are shut down by the Office of Thrift Supervision and transferred to the Federal Deposit

Insurance Corporation, which is named conservator. It becomes the third-largest bank failure in U.S. history. At the time of its seizure, IndyMac Bank has about $1 billion in potentially uninsured deposits held by approximately 10,000 depositors. At the time, the failure is expected to cost the Federal Deposit Insurance Corporation between $4 billion and $8 billion, potentially wiping out more than 10 percent of the regulator's $53 billion deposit-insurance fund.

The director of the Office of Thrift Supervision, John Reich, blamed IndyMac's failure on comments made in June by Senator Charles Schumer. Reich said Schumer gave the bank a "heart attack."

"Would the institution have failed without the deposit run?" Reich asked reporters. "We'll never know the answer to that question."

Monday, July 14, 2008 – U.S. Representative Barney Frank of Massachusetts characterizes mortgage giants Fannie Mae and Freddie Mac as financially sound.

Sunday, September 7, 2008 – The U.S. government seizes mortgage giants Fannie Mae and Freddie Mac, putting the federal government in charge of the two and the $5 trillion in home loans they back. The rescue, announced by Treasury Secretary Henry Paulson and James Lockhart, director of the Federal Housing Finance Agency, throws a lifeline of as much as $200 billion in Treasury support to the two, placing them into conservatorship.

September 14, 2008 — October 3, 2008

Lehman — Après Nous le Déluge

Sunday, September 14, 2008 – Marking one of the most harrowing days in U.S. financial history, Lehman Brothers files for bankruptcy protection after talks aimed at saving the 161-year-old firm break down. As of the close of markets the preceding Friday, Lehman Brothers shares had lost 94 percent of their value on the year. By the close of trading Monday, shares are nearly worthless.

Bank of America agrees to purchase Merrill Lynch for $50 billion. It spells the end of a 94-year-old institution in American finance. At the time of the announcement, Merrill Lynch is Wall Street's third-largest bank. The pairing of the two creates the nation's largest bank by far. The newly minted behemoth surpasses Citigroup, the then-largest bank by assets.

Monday, September 15, 2008 – The Dow Jones Industrial Average plummets more than 500 points, its steepest decline in more than seven years.

Tuesday, September 16, 2008 – American International Group, the world's largest insurer, receives an $85 billion bailout from the U.S. Federal Reserve. In return, the federal government takes an 80 percent stake in the faltering company. It represents the most radical intervention in a private-sector enterprise in the central bank's history.

The bailout is made to prevent the nation's largest insurer from filing for bankruptcy, which would wreak havoc on world markets since AIG has $1.1 trillion in assets and 74 million clients in 130 countries.

Separately, the Reserve Primary Fund "breaks the buck" when its net asset value falls to $0.97, leading to a run on money market funds. Over $140 billion is withdrawn compared with $7 billion the prior week. This leads to a collapse of the commercial paper market, a key source of funding for corporations. Commercial paper is a short-term funding source that helps private companies with daily operations.

Thursday, September 18, 2008 – Lloyds TSB announces it will take over insurer and mortgage lender HBOS. The government will eventually take a 43 percent stake in the enlarged Lloyds Banking Group. U.K. Prime Minister Gordon Brown reassures Sir Victor Blank, then-chairman of Lloyds, that the government would waive competition hurdles if Lloyds were to acquire HBOS, Britain's largest mortgage lender.

Friday, September 19, 2008 – The U.S. Federal Reserve announces it will make funding available to banks and businesses to avert a potential crisis in money markets in a tortuously named program called the Asset-Backed Commercial Paper Money Market Mutual Fund Liquidity

Facility. It will boost general liquidity in the money markets, which hold trillions of dollars on behalf of individuals, pension funds, governments and businesses.

Saturday, September 20, 2008 – The Bush administration asks Congress to spend up to $700 billion to buy up mortgage-backed securities in danger of defaulting. That action would take these debts off the books of banks, hedge funds and pension funds that held them. The legislative proposal represents the most extensive economic intervention by the U.S. government since the 1930s.

Sunday, September 21, 2008 – Goldman Sachs and Morgan Stanley, Wall Street's two last stand-alone investment banks, will become bank holding companies, making them subject to greater regulation by the Federal Reserve. The reclassification continues the biggest restructuring of Wall Street since the Great Depression. It will allow Goldman and Morgan to acquire retail banks and to simplify their borrowing from the Federal Reserve, allowing them access to the Fed's discount window. It is thought the move will keep both entities out of the crosshairs of spooked investors and customers, similar to those who brought down Bear Stearns, Lehman Brothers and Merrill Lynch. The shift will permit the two to create commercial banks that will be able to accept deposits, creating a stable source of funding.

Tuesday, September 23, 2008 – Goldman Sachs announces it will receive a $5 billion cash infusion from Warren Buffett's Berkshire Hathaway in a deal that instills confidence in the banking system. Berkshire will receive preferred stock paying a dividend of 10 percent and warrants to acquire another $5 billion in common stock over five years. Up to now, Buffett has rejected all pleas to aid Wall Street during the current crisis.

Ben Bernanke, Chairman of the U.S. Federal Reserve, and U.S. Treasury Secretary Henry Paulson urge members of the U.S. Senate Banking Committee to approve a $700 billion financial bailout fund.

The U.S. Federal Bureau of Investigation reveals it has been investigating Fannie Mae, Freddie Mac, Lehman Brothers and AIG, along with their executives, as part of a far-reaching investigation into potential mortgage fraud, sources with knowledge of the investigation tell CNN.

Separately, Nomura Holdings, Japan's largest brokerage house, agrees to buy Lehman Brothers' European arm.

Thursday, September 25, 2008 – Washington Mutual Bank, the nation's largest savings and loan, is seized by federal regulators and its assets are sold to JPMorgan Chase. Under the deal, JPMorgan Chase will acquire all the banking operations of WaMu, including $307 billion in assets and $188 billion in deposits. The seizure is directly tied to subprime mortgages and other poor-quality loans.

The collapse becomes the second-largest bankruptcy in U.S. history. To put the size of WaMu's collapse into context, its assets are equal to about two-thirds of the combined book value of the roughly 750 failed thrifts that were sold off by the Resolution Trust Corporation after the savings-and-loan crisis of the late 1980s and early 1990s.

JPMorgan Chase, which scooped up Bear Stearns after its collapse, will pay approximately $1.9 billion to the Federal Deposit Insurance Corporation in the deal after the bank was seized and a quick auction held. After the acquisition, 42 percent of American households would be within 3 miles of a Chase retail bank.

Monday, September 29, 2008 – The U.S. Congress rejects a $700 billion Wall Street financial bailout package. The relief package, intended to invigorate seized lending markets, required 218 votes for passage. It came up 13 votes short, with a final vote of 228 in favor to 205 against. Two-thirds of Democrats and one-third of Republicans voted for the measure.

The news sends the Dow Jones Industrial Average plummeting 778 points, its single-worst point drop ever. The blood-letting erases approximately $1.2 trillion in market value. The S&P 500 index loses 8.8 percent, its seventh worst day on a percentage basis up to that time and the biggest one-day percentage drop since the crash of 1987. The Nasdaq composite falls 9.1 percent, its third-worst day on a percentage basis to that point and its worst decline since the 1987 crash.

"We need to put something back together that works," U.S. Treasury Secretary Henry Paulson said after he and Federal Reserve Chairman Ben Bernanke joined in an emergency strategy session at the White House. On Capitol Hill, Democratic leaders say the House would reconvene in hopes of a speedy vote on a revised version of the bill.

Iceland's government announces the bank Glitnir will be nationalized.

Tuesday, September 30, 2008 – The U.S. Treasury Department changes the federal tax code to encourage bank mergers. It allows a bank to write off all losses of any bank it acquires.

Wednesday, October 1, 2008 – Warren Buffett, the chairman of Berkshire Hathaway, will make a $3 billion investment in General Electric. The move is viewed as a vote of confidence, allaying market fears about the health of its GE

Capital unit. Buffett calls General Electric the "backbone" of American industry. In a live telephone interview from his jet, Buffett tells CNBC's Becky Quick he's seeing more investment opportunities as prices come down. He also repeats his prediction that Congress will pass legislation to help stabilize the nation's credit markets. If not, he predicts, we'll have "terrible, terrible, terrible problems."

Friday, October 3, 2008 – The U.S. Congress passes a reworked version of the Emergency Economic Stabilization Act creating a $700 billion Troubled Asset Relief Program, or TARP, on a 263 to 171 vote, and President George W. Bush quickly signs the bill into law. For passage, Republicans picked up 26 votes in favor of the bill among caucus members who had voted against it in the previous failed vote, while Democrats picked up an additional 32 votes.

Elsewhere, in a surprise announcement, Wells Fargo, the biggest U.S. bank on the West Coast, agrees to rescue Wachovia, including all of its banking operations, in a $14.8 billion transaction requiring no financial involvement from the U.S. government. The announcement comes just four days after Citigroup reached an agreement, in principle, with Wachovia to acquire the latter's troubled banking operations for about $1 a share, at the U.S. government's insistence with a pledge to absorb most of the losses on Wachovia's enormous loan portfolio. The recently passed tax law permitting banks to write off all of an acquired bank's losses allowed Wells to snap up Wachovia, leaving Citi at the altar.

October 4, 2008 – December 19, 2014

The Shakeout

Saturday, October 4, 2008 – British newspapers report on the nationalization of the Icelandic bank Glitnir and the high degree of leverage at Iceland's other big banks.

Monday, October 6, 2008 – The U.S. Federal Reserve signals it will increase the amount available through loans to U.S. banks to $900 billion by the end of the year, increasing the amount the Fed will loan through its so-called term-auction facility by $750 billion.

In an attempt to quell the market contagion, the U.K. government seizes the bank Bradford & Bingley, including its mortgage book. It quickly sells off its retail operations and branches to Spain's Grupo Santander.

Stocks plunge, with the Dow falling as much as 800 points during the session. The S&P 500 index, after falling to its lowest point since September 12, 2003, ended with a loss of 3.6 percent. The Nasdaq composite ends down 4 percent after falling to its lowest point since August 28, 2003, during the session.

Iceland's legislature enacts an emergency law that allows the island-nation's Financial Supervisory Authority to seize control of the nation's financial institutions. In the days that follow, new banks will be founded to assume the domestic operations of the failed Kaupthing, Landsbanki and Glitnir banks, which are put into receivership, resulting in losses for shareholders and foreign creditors. It also means that outside Iceland, more than half a million depositors will lose access to their accounts in foreign branches of Icelandic banks. Iceland's Prime Minister, Geir Haarde, addresses the nation in a speech ending in the phrase: "God bless Iceland."

From 2000 to 2006, Iceland's banks underwent an enormous expansion abroad. It was fueled by ready access to credit in international financial markets, particularly money markets. Iceland's Landsbanki acquired London-based Heritable Bank in 2000. The bank Kaupthing acquired Sweden's JP Nordiska in 2002 and Denmark's FIH Bank in 2004. The same year, Islandsbanki acquired Norway's Kredittbanken and BNBank and merged them into one.

As the crisis progressed, investor confidence in Iceland's banks gradually evaporated, leading to a sharp depreciation of its currency, the króna, in 2008. This increased difficulties for the banks in rolling over short-term debt. By midyear 2008, the nation's external debt was more than 7 times the nation's 2007 gross domestic product. The assets of the three banks totaled more than 11 times its GDP, meaning the Central Bank of Iceland was unable to bail out the country's financial system. As a result, the country suffered a severe economic depression.

Wednesday, October 8, 2008 – The U.S. Federal Reserve, European Central Bank and the central banks of Canada, Britain, Switzerland and Sweden execute a globally coordinated interest rate cut. The move is the latest in a series of unprecedented moves by central banks worldwide to fortify embattled financial markets.

In its most dire forecast in decades, the International Monetary Fund predicts the global economy is primed for a downturn not seen since the 1930s, with the United States and Europe teetering on recession.

Friday, October 10, 2008 – In the first five minutes of trading, the Dow Jones Industrial Average plunges 697 points, falling below 7,900 to its lowest level since March 17, 2003. The benchmark average ends its worst week in its 112-year history with its highest volatility day ever recorded. Over the previous week, it sees its worst weekly decline up to that time on both a point and percentage basis over worries of a worsening credit crisis and worldwide recession.

Saturday, October 11, 2008 – The International Monetary Fund's 185 member countries support a plan of action by the Group of Seven major economies to deal with the credit crisis, calming markets.

Monday, October 13, 2008 – The Dow Jones Industrial Average rallies 936 points, its biggest single-day point gain up to that time and its best day on a percentage basis since 1933. The S&P 500 rallies 104 points, its biggest one-day point gain ever. The Nasdaq's jump of nearly 195 points is the 10th-biggest to that point.

Investors are heartened by the specifics of the $700 billion bank bailout plan, alongside a menu of global initiatives to ease the jittery credit markets. Regulators have been scrambling to fortify financial institutions and allay investor fears that caused credit markets to seize.

Tuesday, October 21, 2008 – The U.S. Federal Reserve announces that it will backstop a private-sector initiative designed to buy commercial paper from money-market mutual funds to provide needed liquidity.

Monday, October 27, 2008 – The U.S. Federal Reserve begins buying so-called commercial paper. It results in greater availability of short-term credit for businesses.

Tuesday, November 4, 2008 – The U.S. Federal Reserve loans $110 billion to Dexia Credit of Belgium and $24.6 billion to the German-Irish Bank Depfa. It is not disclosed until 2011, but one of the great secrets of the financial crisis was that the Federal Reserve allowed heavy discount-window borrowing by non-U.S. banks, regional U.S. banks and other institutions on the brink of ruin.

Wednesday, November 5, 2008 – The International Monetary Fund approves a two-year, $16.4 billion bailout to help the Ukraine government restore economic stability.

Monday, November 10, 2008 – American Express becomes a bank holding company.

Monday, November 17, 2008 – The U.S. Treasury pays out $33.6 billion to 21 banks in the second round of disbursements from the $700 billion bailout fund. It brings the total in payouts to $158.6 billion.

Wednesday, November 19, 2008 – The International Monetary Fund provides a two-year, $2.1 billion bailout for Iceland.

Sunday, November 23, 2008 – Citigroup receives a bailout from the Federal Reserve, U.S. Treasury Department and Federal Deposit Insurance Corporation as the U.S. government agrees to shoulder $306 billion in the bank's toxic assets. In return for the lifeline, the U.S. government receives preferred shares in the bank. U.S. President George W. Bush calls the bailout necessary "to safeguard our financial system," and says the U.S. government would, "if need be," make similar decisions in the future.

Tuesday, November 25, 2008 – The U.S. Federal Reserve announces it will purchase the direct obligations and mortgage-related securities of Fannie Mae, Freddie Mac and Ginnie Mae. It plans to buy as much as $500 billion in mortgage-backed securities and $100 billion in housing agency debt.

Monday, December 1, 2008 – The National Bureau of Economic Research says that the U.S. economy has been in recession since December 2007. The private group of leading economists determines that a peak in economic activity occurred in the U.S. economy in December 2007, marking the end of the expansion that began in November 2001. The expansion lasted 73 months. A previous expansion in the 1990s lasted 120 months.

Tuesday, December 9, 2008 – The Bank of Canada officially declares the Canadian economy in recession. It lowers its key interest rate by half to 1.5 percent, the lowest it has been since 1958.

Thursday, December 11, 2008 – Financier and former Nasdaq chairman Bernard Madoff is arrested in New York in a multibillion-dollar Ponzi scheme. The arrest of the wealth manager, and the revelations that follow, will have far-reaching consequences for banks, individuals, and charities worldwide. The U.S. Securities and Exchange Commission would be roundly criticized for missing the fraud.

Tuesday, December 16, 2008 – The U.S. Federal Reserve sets its key federal funds rate target to a range of between zero and 0.25 percent from its previous rate of one percent. It marks the first time the Fed has cut rates below one percent. The Fed typically sets a target rate instead of a range.

Friday, December 19, 2008 – U.S. President George W. Bush authorizes the Treasury Department to loan up to $13.4 billion to General Motors and $4 billion to Chrysler from TARP funds. The emergency loans are aimed at preventing the collapse of the automakers. The taxpayer lifeline is conditioned on the companies undertaking sweeping changes to demonstrate they can get back to profitability.

Sunday, December 21, 2008 – The government of Ireland announces it will inject 5.5 billion euros into the country's three main lenders. It also announces it will underwrite Bank of Ireland and Allied Irish Banks' plans to raise 1 billion euros each.

Thursday, January 15, 2009 – The Irish government nationalizes Anglo Irish Bank, the nation's third-largest bank, amid fears of collapse. Its shares are suspended the following day.

Friday, January 16, 2009 – The U.S. government throws a new multibillion-dollar lifeline to Bank of America with an additional $20 billion in support from its $700 billion financial rescue fund. The bank agrees to pay an 8 percent dividend on the cash injection and will accept more restrictions on executive pay. The administration, the Federal Reserve and the Federal Deposit Insurance Corporation also agree to participate in a program to provide guarantees against losses on approximately $118 billion in various types of loans and securities backed by residential and commercial real estate. The bulk of these holdings were assumed by Bank of America when it acquired Merrill Lynch.

Sunday, January 18, 2009 – The Danish Parliament unveils an aid package worth 100 billion Danish kroner ($17.8 billion) to bail out Denmark's banks and mortgage lenders. Shares in leading Danish banks will slide the following day despite the news.

Tuesday, January 20, 2009 – Barack Obama is sworn in as the 44th president of the United States as bank shares tumble. Bank of America loses 29 percent, Citigroup falls 20 percent and JPMorgan Chase falls 20.7 percent. The KBW index of banking shares plunges nearly 20 percent to 25.34, its lowest level since 1995. The editorial board of the Christian Science Monitor writes that the four largest U.S. banks "have lost half of their value since January 2."

Friday, January 30, 2009 – Ireland's government debt overtakes Greece's sovereign bonds as the riskiest in Europe, according to credit-default swap prices. Hedging against losses on Irish debt is now more costly than hedging against debt losses of Chile, the Czech Republic, Israel, Malaysia, Saudi Arabia, Thailand and China. Iceland retains the riskiest debt rating.

Wednesday, February 11, 2009 – Ireland says it will bail out two of the nation's largest lenders, Bank of Ireland and Allied Irish Banks, in return for guarantees on lending, executive pay and mortgage arrears. It will take a 25 percent indirect stake in both.

Friday, February 13, 2009 – A sharply divided U.S. Congress approves a $787 billion economic stimulus package to rush emergency government spending and tax cuts to a nation in the grip of a collapsing economy. It hands President Barack Obama a major legislative victory.

Wednesday, February 18, 2009 – The U.S. Federal Reserve adds longer-run projections for the U.S. gross domestic product, unemployment and inflation to their quarterly forecasts in a move seen as effectively creating unofficial inflation targets. House passage on the package came on a 246 to 183 vote, with no support from Republicans.

Thursday, February 19, 2009 – CNBC reporter Rick Santelli unknowingly launches the Tea Party movement when on the floor of the Chicago Mercantile Exchange he calls for a "Tea Party" to oppose the TARP program, bank bailouts and the economic stimulus policies of U.S. President Barack Obama.

Friday, February 27, 2009 – The final report issued by the U.S. Bureau of Economic Analysis revises its U.S. gross domestic product growth rate for the fourth quarter of 2008 to a negative 6.3 percent. The economy contracted at a faster pace than initially estimated in the final months of 2008, according to the government report. The revision points to a deeper recession than first forecast. That was worse than the 3.8 percent drop it reported in its advance report. It was also the worst slowdown since the first quarter of 1982, when gross domestic product fell 6.1 percent.

Separately, the U.S. government announces further involvement in the rescue of Citigroup in a deal that will give the government control over as much as 36 percent of Citigroup's common stock. Financial stocks lead the market downward on economic worries about nationalization, after the government announces that it is expanding its stake in Citigroup. The federal government has already given Citigroup $45 billion in capital, for which it received preferred shares and warrants in the company.

Wednesday, March 4, 2009 – The Obama administration announces new U.S. Treasury guidelines that enable servicers to begin modifications of eligible mortgages under the Administration's Homeowner Affordability and Stability Plan. The Home Affordable Refinance Program, more commonly known by its acronym "HARP," will be part of this program. The latter will be aimed at providing borrowers who may not otherwise qualify for refinancing because of declining home values or reduced access to mortgage insurance the ability to refinance into a lower interest rate or more stable mortgage product or both.

Friday, March 6, 2009 – The Dow Jones Industrial Average reaches a low of 6,469.95, having lost over 54 percent of its value since the October 9, 2007, high. The bear market would clearly reverse course on March 9, 2009, as the Dow rebounded more than 20 percent off its low. By mid-May, the S&P 500 would be up 30 percent and over 60 percent by the end of the year. The duration of this bear market was just short of average due to interventions by governments and central banks to buoy the stock market.

Sunday, March 15, 2009 – Ben Bernanke, chairman of the U.S. Federal Reserve, tells CBS's "60 Minutes" that government officials are laying the groundwork for an economic revival and that a "depression" is avoidable. But he acknowledges that a full recovery will take time and that there are still obstacles. It is the first television interview granted by a sitting Fed chairman in two decades.

Tuesday, April 7, 2009 – Irish Finance Minister Brian Lenihan announces Ireland will create a "bad bank" to buy up toxic assets held by its commercial banks. The National Asset Management Agency will be established six months later, ready to purchase the bad debt.

Friday, May 29, 2009 – Ireland is forced to inject up to $5.6 billion into the now-nationalized Anglo Irish Bank after it experiences the worst loss in Irish banking history.

Tuesday, June 30, 2009 – The second quarter, according to the National Bureau of Economic Research, saw the trough of what came to be known as "The Great Recession." It lasted 18 months from peak to trough. The nadir will set the bottom for a recovery that will last 128 consecutive months to February 2020.

Friday, July 10, 2009 – Calpers, the largest public pension fund in the United States, sues Moody's, Standard & Poor's and Fitch in assigning their highest ratings to securities that later suffered enormous subprime mortgage losses. The suit would not be settled until 2015.

Tuesday, November 10, 2009 – The U.S. Bureau of Labor Statistics reports the October 2009 unemployment rate rose by 0.4 percentage points to 10.2 percent, the highest unemployment rate since April 1983. Since the start of the recession in December 2007, the unemployment rate has grown by 5.3 percentage points. In October, 35.6 percent of unemployed persons were jobless for 27 weeks or more.

Thursday, December 31, 2009 – In 2009, foreclosure documents are filed on 2.8 million properties, up 21 percent from 2008. More than 2.2 percent of all households are in some stage of foreclosure. In Nevada, more than 10 percent of housing units receive at least one foreclosure filing in 2009. Arizona sees the nation's second-highest state foreclosure rate in 2009, with more than 6 percent of its housing units receiving at least one foreclosure filing for the year.

Thursday, January 28, 2010 – The U.S. Senate confirms Federal Reserve Chairman Ben Bernanke for a second term. The 70-30 vote is the smallest margin by which a Fed chairman has won a Senate endorsement in the Fed's 96-year history.

Friday, April 16, 2010 – The U.S. Securities and Exchange Commission charges Goldman Sachs and one of its vice presidents with fraud in allegedly having failed to disclose to investors that one of its mortgage-backed CDOs in 2007, known as "Abacus," was allegedly "designed to fail" by the hedge fund of John Paulson, so that Paulson could rack up hefty profits by betting against it.

Sunday, May 2, 2010 – Debt-stricken Greece receives a bailout of $147 billion from the European Union and the International Monetary Fund. In return, Athens commits itself to spending cuts and tax increases.

Thursday, May 13, 2010 – The Irish government announces it will take an 18 percent stake in Dublin-based Allied Irish Banks, the nation's second-biggest lender by market value. It moves the state closer to taking a controlling stake in the bank.

Wednesday, July 21, 2010 – President Barack Obama signs into law the Dodd-Frank Wall Street Reform and Consumer Protection Act, a bill intended to prevent future financial crises through the increased federal regulation of Wall Street. Both its namesakes received money from the entities they helped regulate: A former Countrywide Financial loan officer told the Wall Street Journal that Senator Chris Dodd knowingly saved tens of thousands of dollars on the refinancing of his two properties in 2003 as part of a special VIP program the California lender had for anyone with the power to influence Fannie and Freddie. Meanwhile, U.S. Representative Barney Frank received a total of $42,350 in campaign contributions directly from Fannie and Freddie, according to the Center for Responsive Politics.

Tuesday, September 14, 2010 – GMAC employee Jeffrey Stephan testifies that he and 13 other employees signed foreclosure-related affidavits they hadn't fully read for files they hadn't fully reviewed. Stephan testifies that he and his team signed approximately 10,000 foreclosure documents a month without verifying their accuracy, as required, or having any knowledge of the cases. He was reportedly given only 1.5 minutes to review each document. The practice will come to be called "robo-signing." The revelation leads to increased scrutiny of foreclosure documentation. GMAC, now called Ally Financial, will halt foreclosures in 23 states. Other big banks will come under fire for the same practices, which will come to be called "*fauxclosures*." These will include JPMorgan

Chase and Bank of America. Federal regulators will later reach a $9.3 billion settlement with 13 banks over the abuses.

Wednesday, November 3, 2010 – The U.S. Federal Reserve launches a second round of quantitative easing, or "QE2," totaling $600 billion in long-term Treasury bonds over the coming eight months to prop up the economy. The central bank also announces it will reinvest an additional $250 billion to $300 billion in Treasuries with the proceeds of its earlier investments.

Thursday, December 23, 2010 – Ireland effectively nationalizes Allied Irish Banks, once the nation's largest bank, with a $4.8 billion capital injection from the country's pension reserves, giving it a 93 percent holding once the bank completes the sale of its Polish interests to Spain's Santander. The Irish government now has unprecedented control over Ireland's banking system, largely wiping out shareholders.

Thursday, January 27, 2011 – The U.S. Financial Crisis Inquiry Commission, a federal fact-finding panel tasked with investigating the crisis, concludes in a scathing 545-page report that the crisis was "avoidable." It contends the crisis was caused by widespread failures in financial regulation, faulting "30 years of deregulation." The report calls out the Federal Reserve's failure to stem the flow of toxic mortgages; it describes a dangerous combination of excessive borrowing and risk by households and Wall Street. The report also faults key policy makers who were ill prepared for the crisis, unable to comprehend the financial system they now regulate, and systemic breaches in accountability and ethics at all levels, describing a banking industry eager to trade in risky subprime mortgages but blind to the attendant dangers.

Wednesday, April 13, 2011 – The U.S. Senate Permanent Committee on Investigations releases the 365-page Levin-Coburn report, "Wall Street and the Financial Crisis: Anatomy of a Financial Collapse." The, report, two years in the making, catalogs conflicts of interest, heedless risk-taking and failures of federal oversight that helped push the country into the deepest recession since the Great Depression. "Using emails, memos and other internal documents, this report tells the inside story of an economic assault that cost millions of Americans their jobs and homes, while wiping out investors, good businesses and markets," said Senator Carl Levin of Michigan.

Wednesday, April 27, 2011 – U.S. Federal Reserve Chairman Ben Bernanke holds the Fed's first ever post-meeting news conference for the first time in the central bank's 98-year history. Bond yields rise after Bernanke speaks.

Monday, August 29, 2011 – The U.S. Federal Reserve announces its plans to keep rates near zero until mid-2013.

Saturday, September 17, 2011 – Protesters begin occupying Zuccotti Park, near Wall Street in Lower Manhattan, where they remain until police expel them two months later. It comes to be known as "Occupy Wall Street."

Wednesday, September 21, 2011 – The U.S. Federal Reserve unveils "Operation Twist," a plan to exchange $400 billion of short-term Treasury bonds on its balance sheet for long-term bonds in an attempt to lower longer-term interest rates.

Thursday, June 28, 2012 – Stockton, California, population 300,000, becomes the largest city to file for bankruptcy protections in U.S. history. The collapse of its housing market and years of fiscal mismanagement leaves the Northern California city unable to pay its workers, retirees and bondholders.

Tuesday, December 10, 2013 – Banking regulators issue final rules for the implementation of the so-called Volcker Rule – a central fixture of the Dodd-Frank Act. The 71-page rule prohibits insured depository institutions and affiliated companies from engaging in short-term proprietary trading of certain securities, derivatives, commodity futures and options for their own account. The Volcker Rule also impose limits on banking entities' investments in, and other relationships with, hedge funds and private equity funds. The rule carves out a considerable number of exceptions.

Friday, December 19, 2014 – The TARP program officially ends as the U.S. Treasury Department sells its remaining shares in Ally Financial, formerly GMAC, offloading its last major investment from the Troubled Asset Relief Program. All told, the program results in a $15 billion profit for the U.S. government, which recoups $441 billion on the $426 billion disbursed. It ends a turbulent chapter, though the moral hazard, layer upon layer of chaotic regulation and banking consolidation the crisis spawned will cost consumers – particularly retirees and those on a fixed income – and small businesses incalculable sums.

Month by Month

In 2001, the U.S. Federal Reserve began cutting the fed funds rate in an effort to stimulate the economy. By 2003, the rate was at one percent. The low rate soon worked its way into the economy, expanding the money supply and stimulating – then overstimulating – the mortgage and real estate markets. Below is a month-by-month breakdown of the crisis that ensued.

Feb 2007   Freddie Mac announces it will no longer buy the riskiest subprime loans, the so-called adjustable-rate "2-28 ARMs." Both Fannie Mae and Freddie Mac assure investors they have little exposure to the subprime market.

Apr 2007   New Century Financial, the largest U.S. nonprime lender, files for bankruptcy.

Jul 2007   The Dow Jones Industrial Average closes above 14,000 for the first time in its history. Investment bank Bear Stearns discloses that two of its subprime hedge funds have lost nearly all of their value.

Aug 2007   French bank BNP Paribas halts
            redemptions on three funds invested in U.S.
            subprime mortgages. Capital One shuts
            down GreenPoint Mortgage. Subprime
            lender Ameriquest closes its doors.

Sep 2007   Britain's Northern Rock bank is thrown a
            lifeline by the Bank of England. It sparks the
            first bank run in the United Kingdom in 140
            years.

Oct 2007   The Dow Jones Industrial Average closes at
            its peak of 14,165. It will not revisit that peak
            for more than five years.

Dec 2007   The U.S. economy peaks.

Jan 2008   Bank of America rescues Countrywide, the
            largest U.S. mortgage lender. The bank will
            lose over $40 billion on the deal. The U.S.
            Federal Reserve cuts the benchmark federal
            funds rate by 75 basis points to 3.5 percent.

Feb 2008   Britain's Northern Rock bank is
            nationalized.

Mar 2008   Teetering on collapse, investment bank Bear
            Stearns is rescued by JPMorgan Chase with
            prodding and financial aid from the U.S.
            government.

Jul 2008   IndyMac Bank fails and is seized by Federal

regulators, making it the largest regulated thrift to fail.

Sep 2008   U.S. seizes mortgage giants Fannie Mae and Freddie Mac. Lehman Brothers collapses. Merrill Lynch is taken over by Bank of America. AIG is given access to as much as $85 billion from the Federal Reserve. The U.S. Treasury backstops money market funds against losses of up to $50 billion. Washington Mutual fails as JPMorgan Chase acquires its deposits and assets. HBOS is taken over by Lloyds. Stocks crater.

Oct 2008   The U.S. Congress passes the Emergency Economic Stabilization Act creating a $700 billion Troubled Asset Relief Program, known by its acronym "TARP." U.S. President George W. Bush signs the bill into law. Wells Fargo rescues Wachovia. U.K. regulators seize Bradford & Bingley.

Nov 2008   The International Monetary Fund approves emergency loans to the Ukraine and Iceland. Fannie Mae and Freddie Mac offload $600 billion in toxic subprime debt to the U.S. government. The U.S. Federal Reserve covertly bails out Dexia Credit of Belgium and the German-Irish Bank Depfa. Citigroup is bailed out.

Dec 2008   General Motors and Chrysler receive bailouts.

Jan 2009   Anglo Irish Bank is nationalized. Barack Obama is sworn in as the 44th U.S. president. Bank of America receives bailout.

Feb 2009 $787 billion U.S. stimulus bill passes and is signed into law. The U.S. government expands stake in Citigroup.

Mar 2009   The Dow Jones Industrial Average hits a market low of 6,469.95, having lost over 54 percent of its value since the October 9, 2007 high.

Jul 2009   The recovery begins. It will last 128 months to February 2020. Calpers, the largest public pension fund in the U.S., sues Moody's, Standard & Poor's and Fitch after the trio assigned their highest ratings to securities that were later downgraded to junk status.

Jul 2010   The Dodd-Frank Wall Street Reform and Consumer Protection Act is signed into law.

The banking crisis and the ensuing financial and real estate crises spawn the worst recession since the 1930s. To paraphrase Mike Campbell, the perennially drunk Scottish war veteran in Hemingway's "The Sun Also Rises," economic crises happen in two ways – gradually, then fast.

The Bailouts

The U.S. government backed up the truck and offloaded pallets of free public cash to institutions that, by all accounts, deserved to fail. It made Ben Bernanke and the Republican Treasury Secretary Hank Paulson seem somewhere to the left of Eugene Debs and the Wobblies. The table below, compiled by the nonprofit news organization ProPublica, combines the $700 billion bailout bill and the separate lifeline to Fannie Mae and Freddie Mac.

Name	Type	Total Disbursed
Fannie Mae	GSE	$119,836,000,000
Freddie Mac	GSE	$71,648,000,000
AIG	Insurer	$67,835,000,000
General Motors	Automaker	$50,744,648,329
Bank of America	Bank	$45,000,000,000
Citigroup	Bank	$45,000,000,000
JPMorgan Chase	Bank	$25,000,000,000
Wells Fargo	Bank	$25,000,000,000

GMAC (later Ally Financial)	Financial Svs.	$16,290,000,000
Chrysler	Automaker	$10,748,284,222
Goldman Sachs	Bank	$10,000,000,000
Morgan Stanley	Bank	$10,000,000,000
PNC Financial	Bank	$7,579,200,000
U.S. Bancorp	Bank	$6,599,000,000
SunTrust	Bank	$4,850,000,000
PHH Mortgage	Mortgage Svs.	$4,739,317,519
Capital One	Bank	$3,555,199,000
Regions Financial	Bank	$3,500,000,000
Wellington Mgt. Legacy Securities PPIF Master Fund	Fund	$3,448,461,000
Fifth Third Bancorp	Bank	$3,408,000,000

Loans from the U.S. Federal Reserve

The money wasn't all free. Some came with strings attached. The U.S. Federal Reserve invented an alphabet soup of loan programs. In early 2010, the Federal Reserve released data on the trillions of dollars behind more than 21,000 loans it made through a dozen emergency programs created during the crisis.

Since its founding, the Federal Reserve has been authorized to lend to banks through its so-called "discount window." In 1932, Congress permitted the Fed, in "unusual and exigent circumstances" to extend credit to individuals, partnerships, and corporations. Somehow, foreign banks were included. The totals below are cumulative. Banks often rolled loans over from one into another, so the amount outstanding at any point in time would likely be less.

Bank	No. of Loans	Cumulative Total
Citigroup	370	$2,427,866,000,000
Merrill Lynch	266	$2,235,585,000,000
Morgan Stanley	246	$2,014,196,000,000
Bear Stearns	71	$962,102,000,000
Bank of America	156	$931,212,000,000
Barclay's	188	$802,004,000,000
Goldman Sachs	138	$782,328,000,000
Royal Bank of Scotland	93	$421,049,000,000
Deutsche Bank	73	$316,630,000,000
Credit Suisse	56	$226,040,000,000
UBS	45	$199,941,000,000
Bank of Scotland PLC	40	$180,920,000,000
Lehman Brothers	28	$170,345,000,000
JPMorgan Chase	46	$161,414,000,000
Wells Fargo	19	$153,953,000,000
Wachovia	23	$147,025,000,000
BNP Paribas	88	$132,615,000,000
Societe General	28	$124,377,000,000
Desdner Bank AG	37	$123,328,000,000
Bayerische Landesbank	37	$108,190,000,000

Gone but not Forgotten...

The Institutions

THEIR SLOGANS WERE all about trust, permanence and can-do spirit: "The power of yes" (Washington Mutual); "You can count on us" (IndyMac); "Where vision gets built" (Lehman Brothers); "Never an unprofitable year" (Bear Stearns). By the end of 2008, they were either holding out tin cups to government or had been wiped cleanly off the map. Their slogans? Hollow bombast that came only to elicit smirks.

Lehman Brothers – Unable to meet investor demands, and with no suitors or lifeline from Uncle Sam, Lehman Brothers, one of America's oldest investment banks, declared bankruptcy on September 14, 2008 – the largest bankruptcy in history. It sent shock waves through the financial system. The panic caused markets to seize in an unprecedented crisis of confidence. But unlike earlier banking panics, this one involved a run by other financial firms, not by individual depositors. The ensuing panic unleashed one of the most severe financial crises in U.S. history. It was a watershed event.

Bear Stearns – In a shotgun marriage, with the Fed and U.S. Treasury Department holding the gun, Bear Stearns, the 85-year-old investment bank, narrowly avoided bankruptcy in its March 16, 2008, sale to JP Morgan Chase at $2 a share. Bear had substantial exposure to mortgages and mortgage derivatives, leading up to the forced marriage. Investors had grown increasingly nervous about its solvency, culminating in a run on the investment bank by its hedge fund clients and other counterparties on March 12, 2008. The problem worsened the next day as the bank lost access to the so-called "repo" market. To quell a wave of investor panic, the Federal Reserve quickly midwifed the acquisition of Bear Stearns by JPMorgan Chase, extending a $30 billion loan to JPMorgan to cover potential losses on Bear's portfolio.

Washington Mutual – When it failed on September 25, 2008, Washington Mutual was the nation's largest thrift (and the sixth-largest FDIC-insured institution). It was also the nation's second-largest holder of payment-option adjustable rate mortgages, so-called "option ARMs." By 2006, the bank had relaxed its lending standards to the point that babysitters and garage musicians were scoring mortgages, claiming salaries worthy of partners at top law firms and vascular surgeons. One mortgage supervisor openly snorted meth at his desk but was known for "getting the job done." The Lehman panic, in no small part, was a catalyst for the downfall of Washington Mutual, with its total assets of $307 billion. It became the biggest bank failure in American history. Its deposits and assets were acquired by JPMorgan Chase.

Wachovia – On September 25, 2008, two large counterparties refused to lend to Wachovia overnight. It spelled Wachovia's doom. On Friday, September 26, "Wachovia Weekend" began. Wachovia's banking assets were the fourth-largest in the United States and it was the largest holder of payment-option adjustable-rate mortgages. The bank informed its lead federal supervisor, the Office of the Comptroller of the Currency, that it would be unable to obtain the funds needed to pay creditor claims. It identified Citigroup and Wells Fargo as potential buyers. On September 29, it was announced Citigroup would acquire Wachovia. The following day, the IRS released Notice 2008-83, which greatly eased the rules for writing off an acquired bank's losses. It allowed Wells Fargo to re-enter the bidding. Wells could now offer a higher share price than Citigroup. Its offer also required no government assistance. On October 3, 2008, Wells Fargo and Wachovia announced the merger agreement.

IndyMac – On July 11, 2008, bank regulators closed Pasadena, California-based IndyMac Bank, a thrift institution with $32 billion in assets and deposits of $19 billion. It came after a long period of almost no bank failures. Between 2005 and 2007, just three U.S. banks failed. The level of media interest in IndyMac's failure was high as a result. In the two weeks after IndyMac's failure, a run on deposits led to the withdrawal of almost $3 billion from the newly chartered bridge institution, IndyMac Federal.

Countrywide – On January 11, 2008, Bank of America rescued the failing Calabasas, California-based Countrywide Financial Corporation, the largest mortgage lender in the United States. It was a deal that would eventually cost Bank of America much more than the $2.5 billion face value of the transaction once the full extent of Countrywide's mortgage losses emerged. The freewheeling Countrywide had been a pioneer in subprime mortgage lending.

Ameriquest – In 2005, Ameriquest Mortgage Company sponsored the Rolling Stones' U.S. tour, but time was not on the subprime lender's side. On August 31, 2007, Ameriquest, once the largest subprime lender in the United States, collapsed. The California-based company styled itself the "proud sponsor of the American dream." Former employees would later give sworn testimony about the lender's tactics, which included concealing interest-rate terms and fees from borrowers, forging loan documents and fabricating incomes. The Rolling Stones weren't the only act whose sticky fingers were graced by the ill-gotten gains generated by Ameriquest. The mortgage company also sponsored professional baseball and football, car racing and Paul McCartney's 2005 Super Bowl performance, and it was a major cash donor to both Democrats and Republicans.

Fannie Mae and Freddie Mac – On September 7, 2008, James Lockhart, the director of the Federal Housing Finance Agency, announced Fannie Mae and Freddie Mac would be placed in federal conservatorship. At the time, Fannie and Freddie were the most highly leveraged financial institutions on the planet, wrote Jason Thomas in National Affairs in a fall 2013 retrospective. Their "lack of diversification and comically inadequate capital base always guaranteed they would fail in any significant housing downturn." Together, the mortgage Godzilla and Mothra owned or guaranteed $5.4 trillion in outstanding mortgage debt. The takeover transferred trillions of dollars in risk directly onto U.S. taxpayers. While Fannie and Freddie were public companies, owned by shareholders, their debt had an implicit government guarantee. It always was – and still is – a recipe for disaster. "The key fact," wrote Peter Wallison of the American Enterprise Institute in USA Today in 2011, "is that, by 2008, before the crisis, half of the 54 million mortgages in the U.S. financial system were subprime and other low-quality mortgages. More than 70 percent of these 27 million weak mortgages were on the books of a government entity, primarily the government-sponsored enterprises Fannie Mae and Freddie Mac." They were ticking time bombs and still lurk in the shadows, unreformed, as a source for future taxpayer liabilities as of this writing in 2020.

The People

THEY COST TAXPAYERS and consumers incalculable sums. What remains is a weird terrarium of former philosopher kings who had reprogrammed the financial circuitry, bucked the received wisdom, refused to hew to fusty notions of prudent stewardship. Their stature was harshly downgraded in the public eye to that of kleptocrat, widow-fleecer, vampire, coddled incompetent, lotus-eater and chief lemming. A few reacted as if they'd been hit on the head with an andiron. Most rode off into the sunset to enjoy a thousand small happinesses. A few still haunt the fetid financial bogs and firths like Japanese water demons.

Richard S. "Dick" Fuld was the final chairman and chief executive officer of Lehman Brothers. As if sparking the largest bankruptcy in American history were not enough, his organization's demise touched off a financial panic that reached all four corners of the globe. "Fuld was the kind of boss who cultivated a cutthroat atmosphere and demanded 24-7 dedication from his deputies," wrote Vicky Ward, author of "The Devil's Casino." Because he failed to recognize signs that the 161-year-old investment bank was on the brink of ruin, he garnered the infamous No. 1 ranking in Portfolio's

"Worst American CEOs of All Time." Unwinding Lehman's $613 billion in outstanding debt spawned an industry unto itself. Don't expect a mea culpa any time soon. Fuld has been largely unrepentant. After the fall, he was spotted undergoing the indignity of commercial aviation – trying to figure out a Jet Blue check-in kiosk at La Guardia.

Angelo Mozilo was the final chairman of the board and chief executive officer of Countrywide Financial. A butcher's son, Mozilo co-founded the company in 1969 and built it into the largest mortgage lender in the country. By the mid-1990s, Countrywide had pioneered a system to shift risk by reselling bundled loans into the secondary market as mortgage-backed securities. These derivatives became a major source of revenue for Countrywide. By the mid-2000s, Countrywide had originated about 15 percent of all home loans in the United States. Mozilo became increasingly dazzled by his company's success and began pursuing the most precarious borrowers. Indeed, about half of Countrywide's loans didn't conform to the criteria needed to be sold to Fannie Mae and Freddie Mac, which was really saying something. It had to sell securitized loans to institutions. His company enabled a class of investments that would bring down the global economy.

James "Jimmy" Cayne was the self-indulgent head of Bear Stearns. Known for leaving the office by helicopter for three-and-a-half-day golf weekends. He was playing bridge when two highly leveraged Bear Stearns hedge funds imploded in July 2007, and was again playing bridge the following March when a liquidity crisis at the firm led to its emergency sale to JPMorgan for less than the value of its Madison Avenue office building. Wrote author Kate Kelly in her book "Street Fighters": "He liked to smoke marijuana. This pastime was well known to some close associates, who had seen him smoking in his Park Avenue apartment. It had also come to the attention of some of the regulars on the bridge circuit, where Cayne was known to retire to his room after the day's play and tuck into his pot stash as a way to relax." The Wall Street Journal also reported on his alleged recreational marijuana use. Cayne denies the allegations. At the time of its forced sale, Bear's share price had tumbled from a high of $170 to a sawbuck. One could say Cayne, at some point, left the building – literally and figuratively. His disengaged management style earned him a spot just behind Ken Lay of Enron in "Portfolio's Worst American CEOs of All Time."

Kathleen Corbet was the president of the ratings agency Standard & Poor's as the firm conferred its top-grade triple-A rating on incomprehensible pools of high-risk loans in return for easy six-figure fees. As one S&P analyst wrote in an email, "[A bond] could be structured by cows and we would rate it." S&P wasn't alone. The other two major players, Moody's and Fitch, did likewise. These perfunctory triple-A ratings coaxed institutional investors into junk-quality derivatives. The parent company, McGraw-Hill, replaced Corbet in August 2007 as criticism of the company's worse-than-useless financial information on subprime-backed products mounted. Much damage was done in the wave of ratings downgrades. They ultimately unleashed mayhem on the markets.

David Lereah was the famously bullish chief economist at the National Association of Realtors, a trade organization. During the run-up, he became one of the world's most recognized housing experts – a poster boy for the infallibility of housing as an investment, from his ubiquitous television interviews to his 2005 book, "Are You Missing the Real Estate Boom?" By 2010, brokers and investors were buying the book for each other as gag gifts. Bloggers nicknamed him "Baghdad Dave," after the Iraqi information minister Mohammed al-Sahaf, called "Baghdad Bob," known for his overly confident press briefings at the time of the U.S. invasion. "I worked for an association promoting housing," Lereah told CNN Money in 2009. "It was my job to represent their interests. I was a public spokesman writing about housing having a good future. I was wrong. I have to take responsibility for that."

Roland Arnall was the owner of Ameriquest Mortgage. By the end of 2005, two of Arnall's companies, Ameriquest and Argent, had funded almost $75 billion in subprime loans. Behind much of this was Arnall's origination of the "stated income loan" – loans approved without income verification. They came to be known as "liar loans." In early 2006, the company announced a $325 million settlement with state attorneys general and agencies in 49 states and the District of Columbia. They had accused Ameriquest of misrepresentation and failing to disclose loan terms, charging excessive fees and inflating appraisals to qualify borrowers for loans. In 2007, Arnall exited the mortgage business, selling most of it to Citigroup for an undisclosed sum. Arnall and his wife, Dawn, were longtime donors to both parties. President George W. Bush later tapped Arnall for an ambassadorship to the Netherlands, recognition from a grateful nation.

Adam Applegarth was at the helm of Northern Rock, one of the United Kingdom's biggest mortgage lenders. He left in December 2007 following the first run on a British bank since 1866. The U.K. government later seized the bank. For many Britons, Northern Rock symbolized the excesses of the financial crisis in the United Kingdom. Throughout the crisis, Applegarth played for Sunderland Cricket Club, an amateur club in the northeast of England. Cricket was his refuge from the day-to-day stresses of running a major bank. The "high risk" business model Northern Rock adopted during his tenure proved to be a very sticky wicket and Applegarth's undoing. He later became famously reclusive, declining all interviews, though he still could be seen on the cricket field.

Kerry Killinger was the final chairman and chief executive officer of Washington Mutual. He was named chief executive in 1990, and chairman in 1991. American Banker named him its 2001 Banker of the Year. He built an empire on "We hope to do to this industry what Wal-Mart did to theirs, Starbucks did to theirs, Costco did to theirs and Lowe's-Home Depot did to their industry," he told the New York Times. "And I think if we've done our job, five years from now you're not going to call us a bank." He was right. In 2012, the FDIC accused him of focusing on short-term gains to increase his own compensation, with a reckless disregard for the bank's long-term safety and soundness. An unrepentant Killinger called the agency's claims "baseless and unworthy of the government" and "political theater."

Stan O'Neal was the celebrated chairman and chief executive of Merrill Lynch. In 2003, O'Neal was promoted from president to chief executive and chairman. He was one of the first African-Americans to hold such a high position on Wall Street. He led Merrill from historically low-risk activities like asset management into the game of creating collateralized debt obligations, which were largely made of subprime mortgage bonds. In order to provide a steady supply of the bonds — the raw material for the derivatives — he allowed

Merrill to load up on the bonds and keep them on its books. He earned $48 million in 2006 and $46 million in 2007. During August and September 2007, Merrill Lynch announced losses of $8 billion due to the huge exposure that Merrill had to subprime mortgage-backed CDOs, and that the firm would have to be sold in order to survive. When he resigned, he left with a severance package including Merrill stock and options worth $161.5 million on top of the $91.4 million in total compensation he'd carried forward from 2006. After Merrill posted the biggest quarterly loss in its 93-year history—and O'Neal was caught approaching Wachovia about a merger without the board's approval—he was bounced from his post. As the subprime market unwound, Merrill went into crisis, and Bank of America swooped in to buy it.

Joe Cassano was the Robinson Crusoe of the so-called credit-default swap – a term that worked its way into the popular lexicon during the meltdown. Cassano created a shadow banking system with these contracts — or wagers — that functioned as insurance policies for the weapons of mass destruction created by the banks. As a founding member of American International Group's notorious Financial-Products unit, Cassano ran the group until he stepped down in early 2008. In good times, AIG's unregulated credit-default-swap business was like shooting fish in a barrel. But those contracts became the mark of death for AIG when the mortgage-backed instruments began to fail. The company required a massive taxpayer rescue totaling nearly $68 billion.

Frank Raines became the first African-American CEO of a Fortune 500 company when he ascended to the helm of mortgage giant Fannie Mae in 1998 from former director of Bill Clinton's Office of Management and Budget. He was a skilled operator in the murky intertidal zone where big business meets big government. It proved lucrative. His total compensation from 1998 through 2004 was a reported $91.1 million, including some $52.6 million in bonuses. Before departing in the midst of an accounting scandal in 2004, he ushered in an era in which Fannie was making big bets on subprime mortgage securities. In December 2006, a government lawsuit accused him and two other Fannie Mae executives of manipulating earnings over a six-year period at the company. In April 2008, he settled with the government. Five months later, Fannie and Freddie were seized by the government and placed into conservatorship.

Davíð Oddsson presided over the collapse of Iceland's banking system, which nearly bankrupted the tiny island-nation. In his two decades as Iceland's longest-serving prime minister and then as central-bank governor, Oddsson, a former mayor of Reykjavik, helped transform Iceland's sleepy economy from one that relied on fishing and aluminum smelting into a whole-of-government financial services powerhouse (think Switzerland, the Cayman Islands or Delaware). Under Oddsson, Iceland privatized its three main banks and floated its currency. Like Viking raiding parties of yore, the newly privatized banks marauded across Britain, snapping up banks and growing massively overleveraged in the process. The International Monetary Fund helped bail out Iceland after its currency lost more than half its value. As of this writing in 2020, Oddsson was co-editor of the daily newspaper Morgunblaðið.

Epilogue

"Boy, that Timberwolf was one *shitty* deal," said the U.S. senator into the mic, otherwise brick-faced and peering over his reading glasses.

Behind the senator's unblinking visage was a glint of mockery; he no doubt delighted in the scatological expletive in the email he'd subpoenaed. A terabyte of subpoenaed emails was poured into the rocker box where the material was sieved and sluiced and run through the baffles. Then this showstopper popped out, and it was clearly the powerful senator's favorite Goldman Sachs email of the day.

"Six hundred million dollars in Timberwolf securities is what you sold. Before you sold it, this is what your sales team was saying about Timberwolf: 'Boy, that Timberwolf was one *shitty* deal.'"

Scatological references are an exceedingly rare and precious thing in Senate committee hearings. So much so, it drew audible gasps, mixed with nervous laughter, from veteran onlookers in the hearing room. It was a benevolent God who provided this email to be read by this senator on this day.

The "Timberwolf" Senator Carl Levin of Michigan was

referring to – or "Timberwolf I CDO" to be exact – was a $1 billion hybrid collateralized debt obligation, a product of its day that included single-A-rated securities from other collateralized debt obligations. Those securities referenced, in turn, residential mortgage-backed securities carrying lower credit ratings, primarily "BBB."

It *was* a turd.

Michael Milken's Drexel Burnham Lambert assembled the first-ever rated collateralized debt obligation in 1987 out of junk bonds Drexel underwrote. It was like the Macintosh II. Everybody had to have one. The thing made sense on paper — pooling many bonds reduced investors' exposure to the failure of any one bond, and putting the securities into tranches enabled investors to pick their preferred level of risk and return.

Wall Street investment banks were snapping up $300,000 mortgages in job lots of 10,000, assembling them into collateralized bonds, getting perfunctory ratings from the Big Three rating agencies and then selling them into the market as $1,000 bonds like pizza slices.

Timberwolf was a confusion of 56 unique collateralized debt obligations that had over 4,500 unique underlying assets. Goldman served as its placement agent, initial purchaser, collateral "put" provider, and liquidation agent. It also hired a hedge fund with former Goldman employees, Greywolf Capital Management, to act as the collateral manager. Greywolf selected the bond's assets with Goldman's approval.

The sharp-elbowed Levin was chairman of the Senate Governmental Affairs Subcommittee on Investigations. It was April 27, 2010.

"Mr. Chairman, [the email] was from the head of the division. Not the sales force," said Daniel Sparks, a former Goldman Sachs Mortgages Department head.

The great inquisitor – his heavy comb-over kept in a style known as a "Fort Myers Shingle" – lowered his chin and narrowed his gaze. This was no time for fine distinctions.

The senator carefully weighed this reply from the one called Sparks, sniffing it for insouciance. It had clearly been a non-answer. And the glib manner in which it was delivered was just the kind of thing that pushed the powerful senator's buttons.

He was here to administer hematomas, but the witness was treating this whole thing as a light dusting. This perceived impudence would not fly.

His stare grew more pinched. His eyes begged … begged … for any sign of weakness. Perhaps he could break the witness, like they do in the movies.

"How much of that *shitty* deal did you sell to your clients after June 22, 2007?" the senator asked, soaking the expletive with an extra layer of contempt. The scatological reference hung in the air, dripping with toxins.

In February 2010, Senator Jim Bunning of Kentucky held up action in the chamber, reportedly telling Democrats: "tough shit." But this repeated use of the expletive seemed to open the floodgate on scatological references in the upper chamber.

"Mr. Chairman, I don't know the answer to that, but the price would have reflected levels they wanted to invest at … at that time…" Sparks replied in another unsatisfying non-answer.

Levin reading from the email: "… July 1, 2007 …. tells the sales force: 'The top priority is Timberwolf.' Your *top* priority to sell is that '*shitty* deal'!"

The senator phrased it not as a question, not as a recitation, but as a declaration. Maybe he could unnerve Sparks, flipping him like a helpless terrapin onto his shell. He eyed the one called Sparks carnivorously.

"*Trying* to sell…" said Sparks blithely.

"Should Goldman Sachs be *trying* to sell a *shitty* deal," the senator cut him off, putting the expletive in play again. There it was – *shitty* deal – today's *spécialité de la maison.*

The chairman was on a tear. Everything was about the expletive referenced in some god-forsaken email that came to light in a subpoena. He flung this term through the air like a bored 12-year-old boy might fling a cow pie on a camping trip. He was trying to cut the witness to ribbons … repent, you white-throated, Mammon-worshipping Wall Street swell!

But "*shitty* deal" didn't begin to describe the thing. Timberwolf's securities began losing value almost as soon as they were purchased. In February 2007, Goldman's Mortgage Department head told a senior executive that Timberwolf was one of two deals "to worry about."

Senator Claire McCaskill of Missouri picked up on the power of the phrase and she, too, invoked the Goldman "*shitty* deal" reference later in the proceeding. It no doubt described the hot mess Goldman and its ilk had helped unleash upon the world's sleepwalking pension fund managers, insurance company executives and assorted widows and orphans.

It wouldn't have been so bad if Goldman hadn't been betting both sides of the trade. They did themselves no favors on that account.

The Timberwolf securities lost 80 percent of their value within five months of being issued. Goldman took 36 percent of the short position in the CDO and made money from that investment. The bank ultimately lost money when it could not sell all of the Timberwolf securities.

But in another vehicle, known as "Abacus," Goldman did not take the short position, but permitted a hedge fund, Paulson & Co. Inc., which reportedly planned on shorting the debt obligation, to play a key but hidden role in selecting its assets. Goldman marketed Abacus securities to its clients, reportedly knowing the debt obligation was designed to lose value and without disclosing the hedge fund's asset selection role or investment objective to potential investors. Three long investors together lost about $1 billion from their Abacus investments, while the Paulson hedge fund was reported to have profited by about the same amount.

Since about the mid-1990s, a complex sausage-making process had materialized on Wall Street that started with home loans made to individual borrowers. Most home loans entered the pipeline soon after borrowers signed the documents.

Loans were put into packages and sold off in bulk to securitization firms – including investment banks such as Merrill Lynch, Bear Stearns and Lehman Brothers, and to commercial banks and thrifts like Citibank, Wells Fargo, and Washington Mutual. The firms would package the loans into residential mortgage–backed securities that would mostly be stamped with triple-A ratings by the credit rating agencies, and sold to investors.

In many cases, the securities were repackaged again into collateralized debt obligations, so-called "CDOs" – often composed of the riskier portions of these securities – which would then be sold to other investors. Most of these securities would also receive the coveted triple-A ratings that investors believed attested to their quality and safety. Some investors would buy an invention from the 1990s called a credit default swap to protect against the securities' defaulting. For every buyer of a credit default swap, there was a seller. There had to be. As these investors made opposing bets, the layers of entanglement in the securities market increased.

Soon, everyone's Aunt Agnes was using terms like "structured finance," "senior tranche" and "credit default swap." These terms – associated with pestilential assets – had entered the national lexicon as the financial markets imploded in 2008. In a nutshell, structured finance was the mechanism by which subprime and other mortgages were turned into complex investments. A triple-A rating most often consecrated the issuance in what smacked of a payola arrangement by the credit-rating agencies.

The instruments grew more and more complex and incomprehensible; CDOs were constructed out of CDOs, creating CDOs squared. When firms ran out of real product, they started generating cheaper-to-produce "synthetic CDOs" — composed not of real mortgage securities but just of bets on other mortgage products. Each new permutation allowed bond underwriters to extricate additional fees and trading profits. And each new layer brought in more investors betting on the mortgage market, even after the market had started to turn.

By the time the whole thing came crashing down, a mortgage on a home in Modesto, California, might become part of dozens of securities owned by hundreds of clueless investors or parts of bets being made by hundreds more. Obama administration Treasury Secretary Timothy Geithner, the president of the New York Federal Reserve Bank during the crisis, described the resulting product as "cooked spaghetti."

***

The market-destroying actions of the system – from those of delusional homeowners to hives of venal mortgage brokers to marauding executives at nonbank lenders to rapacious Wall Street investment bankers and conveniently incompetent credit-rating agencies – were absurd and perfidious enough to eclipse most anything dispensed by Mother Nature. The theory of biological markets would be hard-pressed for a simile. One thing was clear: Wall Street was supercharging the behavior, while U.S. federal meddling to increase homeownership rates and draconian rate cuts by the Fed years earlier also contributed to this unholy mess.

To find a simile in the animal kingdom required a very dark turn. This was too weird for the theory of biological markets. It was more a parasite-host story.

One of the planet's most bizarre natural phenomena is the suicidal mind-control exerted on carpenter ants by a fungus in the jungles of Brazil. The fungus can turn an ant into a zombie. Maybe this was an apt metaphor for how mortgage originators came to be controlled by Wall Street. It no doubt was the inspiration for the 2014 post-apocalyptic novel "The Girl with all the Gifts."

When the fungus Ophiocordyceps unilateralis infects a carpenter ant, it invades muscle fibers throughout the ant's body over the span of about a week. It hijacks the creature's mind and taps into its nutrients; the body-snatcher then compels the ant to climb vegetation to a height of exactly 9.842 inches – no more and no less. (It's actually 25 centimeters, which seems to confirm that carpenter ants have embraced the metric system.) This height puts it at a level off the jungle floor that allows for the ideal temperature and humidity for the fungus to thrive. The crazed ant bites into the underside of a leaf or a twig with its powerful mandibles and then weakens.

The ritual ends with the ant dying and sprouting a spore-laden mushroom from its head. This ghastly fruiting body releases infectious spores onto the ground below, where they will infect other foraging ants.

There are other parasites that manipulate their hosts in this way. An unsettling flatworm called the Euhaplorchis californiensis forms a latticework over the brain of the aptly named California killifish, leaving the brain intact while forcing the fish to behave erratically and draw the attention of birds—the flatworm's next host.

No institution had done more to destroy a vital firewall than the credit-rating firms: Moody's, Standard & Poor's and Fitch. They *were* the vital firewall, the last outpost before the frontier. The system was wired to rely on the three firms. Without their massive rubberstamping of the once rare triple-A rating, the 2007-2008 financial crisis doesn't happen. Hard stop.

The Financial Crisis Inquiry Commission's report examined breakdowns at the credit-rating firm Moody's. From 2000 to 2007, Moody's proprietary "black box" modeling algorithms spit out triple-A ratings for nearly 45,000 mortgage-related securities. To put that in perspective, in early 2010, there were just six private-sector companies in the entire United States that carried this coveted rating.

In 2006 alone, Moody's put its triple-A imprimatur on mortgage-related securities every working day. The results were calamitous: 83 percent of the mortgage securities rated triple-A that year were later downgraded.

Typically, investments holding triple-A ratings have had a less than 1 percent probability of default. But in 2007, the vast majority of residential mortgage-backed securities with triple-A ratings suffered substantial losses; some failed outright. Analysts have determined that over 90 percent of the triple-A ratings given to subprime mortgage-backed securities originating in 2006 and 2007 were later downgraded to junk status.

In August 2007, German Chancellor Angela Merkel criticized the credit-rating agencies, presciently identifying the white-hot center of the rot that was only beginning to be exposed.

The virulent sludge at the heart of the crisis could not have been marketed and sold without their stamp of approval. Investors relied on the Big Three credit-rating agencies, often blindly and in good faith. In some cases, they were obligated to use them, or regulatory capital standards hinged on their top ratings. Their ratings helped the market soar and their downgrades through 2007 and 2008 cut a wide swath of economic destruction.

Investors and financial institutions holding the triple-A-rated securities saw their values evaporate. It didn't take long before widespread losses led to a loss of confidence in the institution of the triple-A rating, in the holdings of major financial institutions and, ultimately, in the dependability of U.S. financial markets.

Levin's subcommittee examined a $1.1 billion collateralized debt obligation underwritten by Deutsche Bank known as "Gemstone 7," which issued securities in March 2007. It was one of 47 such investment vehicles totaling $32 billion that Deutsche Bank underwrote from 2004 to 2008. Deutsche Bank made $4.7 million in fees from Gemstone 7, while the collateral manager, a hedge fund called HBK Capital Management, was slated to receive $3.3 million. Gemstone 7 concentrated risk by including within a single financial instrument 115 residential mortgage-based securities whose financial success depended upon thousands of high-risk, poor-quality subprime loans. Many of those securities carried triple-B, or even double-B ratings, making them among the highest-risk securities sold to the public.

Nearly a third contained subprime loans originated by Fremont, Long Beach and New Century, lenders well known within the industry for issuing poor-quality loans, the Levin-Coburn report found. Deutsche Bank also sold securities directly from its own inventory to the Gemstone 7. Deutsche Bank's trading desk knew that many of these residential mortgage-based securities were likely to lose value, but did not object to their inclusion in Gemstone 7, even securities that Deutsche Bank's top global trader Greg Lippmann was openly calling "crap" or "pigs." Despite the poor quality of the underlying assets, Gemstone's top three tranches received triple-A ratings.

All the perfunctory triple-A credit ratings introduced risk into the U.S. financial system. It was a major cause of the financial crisis, found the Levin-Coburn report. In addition, the July 2007 mass downgrades set off the collapse of the residential mortgage-backed security and CDO markets, and, likely more than any other single event, but for the Lehman collapse, epitomized the crisis.

What happened at the rating agencies was a scandal within a scandal, brought on by flawed computer models, client pressure, the relentless drive for market share and the absence of accountability.

As Upton Sinclair once wrote, "It is difficult to get a man to understand something when his salary depends upon his not understanding it."

The new alchemy known as "structured finance" could not have been sold without ratings by the Big Three rating agencies. The charters and bylaws of many money markets and pension funds required them to hold only the safest securities – those designated by the ratings agencies as "triple-A."

The Department of Labor restricts pension fund investments to securities rated "A" or higher. Credit ratings affect even private transactions: contracts may contain triggers that require the posting of collateral or immediate repayment, should a security or entity be downgraded. The high credit ratings functioned as the connective tissue.

In July 2007, as mortgage delinquencies intensified and mortgage-backed securities began incurring losses, Standard and Poor's and Moody's abruptly reversed course and began downgrading hundreds and then thousands of their debt obligation ratings, some less than a year old. Triggers played a big role in the financial crisis and helped cripple AIG.

Before the big mortgage-securitization craze, the credit rating agencies had mainly helped investors evaluate the safety of municipal and corporate bonds and commercial paper. Although evaluating probabilities was their stock-in-trade, they found that rating these tricky mortgage-backed securities required a new type of analysis.

Participants in the securitization industry realized that they needed to secure favorable credit ratings to sell structured products to investors.

"The rating agencies were important tools to do that because you know the people that we were selling these bonds to never really had any history in the mortgage business. They were looking for an independent party to develop an opinion," Jim Callahan told the Financial Crisis Inquiry Commission. Callahan is CEO of PentAlpha, which services the securitization industry, and years ago he worked on some of the earliest securitizations.

Investment banks paid handsome fees to the rating agencies, which, feigning even-handedness, could be counted upon to reliably spit out triple-A ratings.

From the mid-1990s, Moody's rated tranches of mortgage-backed securities using one of three models. The first, and probably least worthless of the trio, was developed in 1996. It rated residential mortgage-backed securities. In 2003, Moody's created a new "black box" – dubbed the "M3 Prime" – to rate prime, jumbo and Alt-A deals. In the fall of

2006, when the housing market had already peaked, it developed its model for rating subprime products. It was called the "M3 Subprime."

The models incorporated firm- and security-specific factors, market factors, regulatory and legal factors, and macroeconomic trends. The M3 Prime let Moody's automate more of the process. Moody's didn't sample or review individual loans. The firm used loan-level information from the issuer. Relying on loan-to-value ratios, borrower credit scores, originator quality, loan terms and other information – some of which turned out to be rubbish – it simulated the performance of each loan in 1,250 scenarios, including variations in interest rates and state-level unemployment, as well as home price changes. On average, across the scenarios, home prices trended upward at about 4 percent annually.

The model put little weight on the possibility prices would fall sharply nationwide. Jay Siegel, a former Moody's team managing director involved in developing the model, told the federal commission, "There may have been [state level] components of this real estate drop that the statistics would have covered, but the 38 percent national drop, staying down over this short but multiple-year period, is more stressful than the statistics call for."

Even as housing prices rose to unprecedented levels, Moody's never adjusted the scenarios to put greater weight on the possibility of a decline. According to Siegel, in 2005, "Moody's position was that there was not a ... national housing bubble."

What Siegel next told members of the federal commission was perhaps the most shocking revelation. After a given security had been run through one of Moody's automated ratings models, actual human judgment was involved and actual humans could have intervened. The lead analyst on a given security convened a rating committee made up of analysts and managers to assess it and determine the overall ratings for the securities.

"One common misperception is that Moody's credit ratings are derived solely from the application of a mathematical process or model. This is not the case... The credit rating process involves much more — most importantly, the exercise of independent judgment by members of the rating committee. Ultimately, ratings are subjective opinions that reflect the majority view of the committee's members."

As Roger Stein, a Moody's managing director, noted, "Overall, the model has to contemplate events for which there is no data."

Moody's officials told the inquiry commission they recognized that stress scenarios were not sufficiently severe, so they applied additional weight to the most stressful scenario, which reduced the portion of each deal rated "triple-A." Stein, who helped develop the subprime model, said the output was manually "calibrated" to be more conservative to ensure predicted losses were consistent with analysts' "expert views." Stein also noted Moody's concern about a suitably negative stress scenario; for example, as one step, analysts took the "single worst case" from the M3 Subprime model simulations and multiplied it by a factor in order to add deterioration.

Moody's did not sufficiently account for the deteriorating quality of the loans being securitized. Its former managing director Jerome Fons described the problem:

"I sat on this high-level structured-credit committee, which you'd think would be dealing with such issues [of declining mortgage-underwriting standards], and never once was it raised to this group or put on our agenda that the decline in quality that was going into pools, the impact possibly on ratings, other things. We talked about everything but, you know, the elephant sitting on the table."

To rate one security called the "CMLTI 2006-NC2," Moody's first used its model to simulate losses in the mortgage pool. Those estimates, in turn, determined how big the junior tranches of the deal would have to be in order to protect the senior tranches from losses. In analyzing it, the lead analyst noted it was similar to another Citigroup security of New Century loans that Moody's had rated earlier and recommended the same amount. Then the deal was tweaked to account for certain riskier types of loans, including interest-only mortgages.

For its efforts, Moody's was paid an estimated $208,000 (S&P also rated this deal and received $135,000.) Three tranches of this deal would be downgraded less than a year after issuance – part of Moody's mass downgrade on July 10, 2007, when housing prices had declined by only 4 percent. In October 2007, the M4–M11 tranches were downgraded and by 2008, all the tranches had been downgraded.

The 2015 film "The Big Short," based on a book of the same name by Michael Lewis, nails it. A jerky hand-held camera captures Georgia, a fictional executive at Standard & Poor's at 25 Broadway. In a less-than-subtle dig at the rating agency's institutional myopia, the character is wearing wrap-around post-dilation sunglasses after visiting her eye doctor.

"My eye doctor's always busy … I end up taking any appointment they'll give me … my whole morning gets shot to hell!" she apologizes to Mark Baum, played by Steve Carell.

"We don't understand why the ratings agencies haven't downgraded subprime bonds since the underlying loans are clearly deteriorating," says a gum-chewing Vinny Daniel, played by Jeremy Strong, to the S&P woman. The two visitors work for Greenwich, Connecticut-based FrontPoint Partners, a unit of Morgan Stanley. Carell's character is a thinly veiled portrayal of Steven Eisman, who rose to fame betting against collateralized debt obligations.

"Well … the delinquency rates do have people worried but they're actually within our models," she tells him.

"So … you're convinced the underlying mortgages in these bonds are solid loans?" asks Baum.

"That is our *opinion*, yes," says the S&P woman.

"Have you looked at the loan-level data?" asks Vinny.

"Excuse me, sir, what do you think we do all day?" protests Georgia.

"Georgia, have you ever refused to rate any of these bonds' upper tranches 'triple A'? Can we see the paperwork?" asks Baum.

Exasperated, she explains the lay of the land to the two in the way one explains something to a complaining but faultless child.

"If we don't give them the ratings, they'll go to Moody's right down the block," says the S&P woman. "If we don't work with them, they will go to our competitors. It's not our fault. It's just the way the world works … and I never said that. … and it is not my decision. I have a boss."

The film turned on this scene.

In late 2006, high-risk mortgages began incurring delinquencies and defaults at an alarming rate, reported U.S. Senate investigators in the congressional April 2011 report "Wall Street and the Financial Crisis: Anatomy of a Financial Collapse." Despite signs of a deteriorating mortgage market, Moody's and S&P continued for six months to issue investment-grade ratings for numerous residential mortgage-backed securities and collateralized debt obligations.

Masquerading as even-handed observers acting on high

moral principle, the credit-rating agencies played along.

By the end of 2009, over half of the collateralized debt obligations by value issued from 2005 to 2007 given a triple-A rating were later downgraded to "junk" or suffered a "principal loss" (which means investors not only forfeited interest payments but lost some or all of their principal). In the case of Moody's alone, of all mortgage-backed securities it had rated triple-A in 2006, it downgraded 73 percent to "junk," a U.S. government inquiry found. The consequences would reverberate throughout the financial system.

It somehow escaped the Big Three ratings agencies that mortgage underwriting standards in America had deteriorated to the point that between 2002 and 2007, an estimated $3.2 trillion in loans were made to homeowners with bad credit and undocumented incomes.

"If the government outsourced drivers' licenses, and the roads filled with accidents caused by bad drivers, it would stop using those companies. Congress should do the same with the credit rating agencies," wrote U.S. Securities and Exchange Commission Commissioner Kathleen Casey in the New York Times.

"But as the reliance on ratings has spread, their reliability has plummeted. A continuous thread runs through the collapse of Orange County, Enron, Bear Stearns and the issuers of collateralized debt obligations: All received high ratings and then promptly collapsed."

She lamented in 2009 that although many of their ratings turned out to be catastrophically misleading, the large rating agencies enjoyed their most profitable years ever during the past decade.

Even in 2009, in the smoldering wreckage, issuers and underwriters almost always returned to the large rating agencies.

"They do so for a very simple reason — because there is nowhere else for them to go," said Casey. "For those who still believe in free-market capitalism, the continued dominance of a critically important industry by just a few firms is an unfortunate reality."

Economist Joseph Stiglitz weighed in the same year.

"If the banks were the main perpetrators of the crime, they had many accomplices. Rating agencies played a central role." They became masters of financial alchemy, their automated models magically converting F-rated subprime mortgages into A-rated securities that were safe enough to be held by pension funds.

"This was important, because it allowed a steady flow of cash into the housing market, which in turn provided the fuel for the housing bubble," wrote Stiglitz. "The rating agencies' behavior may have been affected by the perverse incentive of being paid by those that they rated, but I suspect that even without these incentive problems, their models would have been badly flawed. Competition, in this case, had a perverse effect: It caused a race to the bottom—a race to provide ratings that were most favorable to those being rated."

In April 2009, the nation's largest public pension fund filed suit in California state court linked to $1 billion in losses that it says stemmed from "wildly inaccurate" credit ratings from the three ratings agencies. Ohio's attorney general filed suit against the rating agencies for "false and misleading ratings" on losses to its state retirement fund of $457 million. In 2013, Moody's and Standard & Poor's settled two lawsuits accusing the rating agencies of misleading investors about the safety of risky debt vehicles that they had rated. The Calpers suit dragged on and wasn't fully settled until 2015. In the end, the Big Three rating agencies became cauldrons of empty, commission-driven deal-making – financial onanism. They peddled dangerously misleading financial information to the world's proverbial widows and orphans.

The male scorpion fly, named for its curved, scorpion-like tail, engages in a similar pay-to-play arrangement, offering the female of the species an exchange commodity of a fresh kill or a valuable wad of saliva in return for sex.

The writings of Thomas Malthus and Adam Smith were said to have influenced Charles Darwin, but only recently have evolutionary theories influenced economics.

A variety of ant runs a protection racket against the lycaenid butterfly. Its larvae pays off the ants in the form of a sweet fluid it excretes. In exchange for the commodity, the ants then protect the caterpillars from predators.

The relatively recent notion of "biological markets" views behavior in the animal kingdom through the economic prism of supply and demand to predict the trade-value of commodities exchanged between trader classes – even when those trader classes are winged, furry or covered with mucus.

"Biological markets are all over the place," Ronald Noë, a Dutch biologist at the University of Strasbourg, told Bloomberg. He first proposed the concept of the biological market in 1994.

Noë's theory provides a framework for grasping cooperative interactions within and between species. In a biological market, members of the animal kingdom evaluate their options and make choices that result in the highest payoff with the least risk.

Finding an apt simile for the 2007-2008 human financial crisis may require going into the Mariana Trench – quite literally.

The anglerfish is a hideous creature. The deep-sea variations have large heads and crescent-shaped maws lined with enormous fangs that angle inward. Their translucent and covered with mucous. And in an adaptation to the dark, frigid world that is the deep ocean, their stomachs are highly expandable. It allows them to take advantage of every prey opportunity that comes along. Most female anglerfish run between about 1 to 7 inches, with a few variants growing as long as several feet.

The adult females have a modified dorsal ray extending from their foreheads – it resembles a fishing rod. At its tip is a glowing organ filled with luminescent bacteria. Anglerfish can waggle the organ or pulse light to it to attract pelagic crustaceans, fish, and other prey.

When an anglerfish opens its enormous gash, the resulting suction, and then the fangs, draw in the hapless shrimp, squid or lanternfish. After the brute's maw slams shut, tiny, inward-angled teeth in the gullet deposit the quarry into the fish's elastic belly.

The anglerfish can't be arsed to hunt the conventional way. Instead it relies on an elaborate fishing rod to lure in prey. But the gods, in their wisdom, furnish a corrective to the anglerfish's built-in advantage.

In 1833, a specimen, a female, washed ashore in Greenland and caused a minor sensation. When scientists first began examining anglerfish – mostly dead or dying specimens from fishing nets – they noticed all were female.

Scientists soon became aware that some of the females had hideous parasites attached to them. The "parasites" turned out to be highly reduced males. Young male anglerfish face enormous odds against finding a partner in the vast abyss, so when a male is able to locate a female, the suitor bites onto the female's belly. In the process, the male releases an enzyme that digests the skin of his mouth and her body.

The act fuses the pair permanently in a state of unholy matrimony. Their tissues and circulatory systems intertwine.

Next, the male's eyes and fins atrophy away. The beau will live out the rest of his days nourished by the female's blood, but breathing with his own gills and still capable of producing sperm. The males appear to have evolved for a single purpose – locate a female, become one with it and deliver sperm.

More than one male could be fused onto a single individual female. It was not uncommon with some anglerfish species to be hijacked by up to eight males. This was a strange business.

This monstrous sight, a beast using a fishing rod to mesmerize its prey while members of its own species glommed onto it, reminds one of the exotic borrower enticements, stimulated by the bioluminescence, the voracious loan originators and the Wall Street banks, along with Fannie and Freddie, all fused onto the brute for the ride. It was a Hail Mary, but maybe this was the biological paradigm!

***

The Federal National Mortgage Association, more commonly known as "Fannie Mae," was founded in 1938 by an act of Congress. The "federal instrumentality" would help provide a steady flow of cash to jittery banks, savings and loans, and mortgage companies that made home loans. It helped free up a seized mortgage market during the Great Depression.

But Fannie wasn't dismantled when the Great Depression ended. Nor did it settle into comfortable obsolescence. It only expanded. In 1968, it was taken public. Its New Deal bona fides and implicit federal backstop allowed it to be seen through a scrim of quasi-governmental legitimacy while it became absurdly undercapitalized. Because it wasn't actually a government entity, it could never be properly ventilated. It would become an agent of contagion.

Like other publicly traded companies, Fannie and Freddie – the latter came along in 1970 – had to be competitive to maintain their share prices, but unlike fellow publicly traded companies, their federal charters brought them big, unfair advantages due to lower operating and funding costs (such as a line of credit with the U.S. Treasury) and an implied U.S. taxpayer backstop. The twin mortgage companies learned they could privatize profits while collectivizing risks. They grew into sasquatches.

The two were often lauded as paradigms of public-private partnerships – that is, the harnessing of private capital to advance the social goal of expanding homeownership.

When pushed to do more toward their societal mandate, they could stress their duty to shareholders as profit-seeking enterprises. If share prices slumped or if executives ran afoul of regulations, they could plead their public mission. They could be wet fingers in the wind. When under attack, Fannie and Freddie would call in markers with friends on Wall Street, on Capitol Hill and in the housing lobby. They became independent caliphates operating within U.S. borders.

Under attack, they would shapeshift and become obstreperous. Their propaganda arms would go into high gear as they became paragons of virtue and probity and appealed to the public's high-mindedness.

"Don't bother us with your allegations of accounting irregularities and illegal political fundraising. We're too busy serving hot breakfasts to underprivileged kids in our parking lot!"

Fannie and Freddie's activities take two broad forms. First, their credit-guarantee business involves the creation of residential mortgage-backed securities by purchasing a pool of conforming mortgages from originators — typically banks or nonbank lenders — and then issuing a security that receives cash flows from the mortgage pool. In return for this guarantee, the firms receive a monthly "guarantee fee," effectively an insurance premium coming out of the borrower's interest payment.

Second, the firms' "portfolio investment" business involves holding and financing assets on their own balance sheets, including whole mortgages, their own agency mortgage-backed securities, non-agency mortgage-backed securities, and other types of fixed-income investments. Fannie Mae and Freddie Mac largely fund these assets by issuing "agency" debt.

Their many advantages over private-label competitors – the investment banks that learned how to buy, securitize and sell off U.S. mortgage debt – created a kind of malignant narcissism at Fan and Fred. This was on top of the virtue-signaling and preening over the political whims of the moment to please their patrons in government. Their respective politburos were always reliable on that account.

Two past episodes served to create a perception in financial markets that Fannie's and Freddie's debt and mortgage-backed securities were implicitly government guaranteed. These episodes incentivized them to hold less capital to support their mortgages. Fannie and Freddie leveraged these advantages over their Wall Street rivals for many years to become big, profitable and politically powerful.

The profitability and the predictability promised a low-risk, well-paying – if somewhat boring – existence for Fannie and Freddie employees.

"But in reality," reported the New York Fed in a March 2015 report, "the hybrid structures of Fannie Mae and Freddie Mac were destined to fail owing to their singular exposure to residential real estate and moral hazard incentives based on the implicit guarantee of their liabilities."

The two are exempt from U.S. bankruptcy code but may be placed into "conservatorship" should they fail, which happened in September 2008.

From 2008 to 2011, Fan and Fred posted total combined losses (in terms of comprehensive income) of $266 billion and required a combined $190 billion injection of taxpayer funds from the U.S. Treasury. As of press time, the money wasn't close to being repaid. The biggest contributor to the losses was credit guarantees on toxic single-family mortgages, reported the New York Fed in 2015.

But do not feel sorry for Fannie or Freddie even in conservatorship. Fannie Mae realized an incredible $1.9 million of profit for each of its 7,500 employees in 2019, according to Digital Information World. Its brother, Freddie Mac, took the third spot at $1 million per employee.

The 2015 New York Fed report concludes that placing Fannie and Freddie into conservatorship had so far failed to produce reform of the U.S. housing finance system.

Fannie and Freddie both had multibillion-dollar accounting scandals that stunned Wall Street and brought record civil fines against them in settlements with the government. In 2004, the Office of Federal Housing Enterprise Oversight, the Justice Department and the Securities and Exchange Commission alleged accounting fraud at Fannie Mae that included manipulations of earnings, allowing top company executives to pocket hundreds of millions in bonuses from 1998 to 2004. There were shareholder lawsuits, too. The suits were later settled.

By the mid-2000s, Fannie and Freddie were heavily involved with subprime lending. The loans began to sour in 2008. During the 2nd quarter of 2008 alone, the two lost a combined $3.1 billion. Half of their credit losses came from Alt-A stated-income loans, called "liar loans" – mortgages made without proof of the borrower's income or assets. The worst carried the nickname "ninja loans," short for "no income, no job, and (no) assets."

Many of the lenders that specialized in such loans are now defunct or have changed their names – American Home Mortgage, Ameriquest, Countrywide, GMAC and IndyMac Bank.

In April 2007, Freddie Mac was fined $3.8 million by the Federal Election Commission as a result of illegal political fundraising, much of it benefiting members of the influential United States House Committee on Financial Services, which oversees the mortgage guarantor.

Frank Raines was at the helm of mortgage giant Fannie Mae since 1998. Before departing in the midst of the accounting scandal, he ushered in an era in which Fannie was making big bets on subprime mortgage securities. His total compensation from 1998 through 2004 was a reported $91.1 million, including some $52.6 million in bonuses. In December 2006, a government lawsuit accused him and two other Fannie Mae executives of manipulating earnings over a six-year period at the company. In April 2008, Raines settled with the government. Five months later, Fannie and Freddie were seized by Uncle Sam, wiping out shareholders.

In late February 2007, Fannie Mae and Freddie Mac reassured investors they had little exposure to the subprime mortgage market.

"Fannie and Freddie failed in large part because they made bad business decisions and held insufficient capital," concluded the left-leaning Center for American Progress in a report in 2012.

Fannie and Freddie's embrace of toxic mortgages culminated in the case of Addie Polk, 90. Polk was an African-American widow who shot herself twice in the chest during a

Fannie Mae-initiated eviction action. A mortgage had been pushed on the elderly Akron, Ohio, woman, devouring all equity in a home she and her late husband had owned free and clear.

In 2001, the retiree was persuaded to take out a $46,000 mortgage on the house, which was reported to be worth less than half the loan amount. Three years later, she was reportedly pressured to refinance for another loan of $45,620, as well as an $11,380 line of credit. Only when the elderly Polk shot herself and her case made the wire services did Fannie announce it would halt its eviction of the elderly widow. Her story was retold in the 2020 docuseries "The Con" by filmmakers Eric Vaughan and Patrick Lovell.

For many, Polk's case came to symbolize the way in which nonbank lenders, enabled by Fannie and Freddie, were targeting vulnerable borrowers in underserved neighborhoods.

In Polk's case, the filmmakers seemed to be reporting on an affinity scam, defined as a hustle in which fraudsters prey upon members of identifiable religious and ethnic groups, language minorities, elderly or practitioners of certain professions. It's one reason why Bernie Madoff was so effectively able to defraud Jewish Americans or why a pastor from Oaxaca, Mexico, might have a leg-up in selling subprime loans to Oaxacan transplants in California's Central Valley.

In their book "Predatory Lending and the Destruction of the African-American Dream," write law professors Janis Pearl Sarra and Cheryl Wade:

"Millions of middle-class and high-income African Americans who qualified for regular fixed-rate, long-term mortgages were steered to subprime mortgages. For the most part, white American borrowers who had credit histories identical to the credit histories of African-American borrowers were not targeted for subprime mortgages."

There has been backsliding in the decade since the crisis. Enabled by Fannie Mae, Freddie Mac and the Federal Housing Administration, commission-driven salesmen are again descending on equity-rich but cash-poor neighborhoods, helping homeowners deplete precious home equity accumulated since the 2007-2008 carnage.

In 2020, the Oakland, California-based Greenlining Institute, a nonprofit public policy and advocacy group, found that the eight largest nonbank mortgage lenders in California lent a disproportionate amount of their portfolios to black and Hispanic home buyers when compared with the more regulated chartered banks in the state. There are many open questions about what this means. That year, U.S. Department of Housing and Urban Development Secretary Ben Carson told the publication American Banker about 85 percent of federally insured mortgages were now being originated by non-depository institutions, up from the already high 50 percent prior to the financial crisis.

The radioactive practices of nonbank lenders in the lead-up to the meltdown were described by the martyred Lehman global fixed-income chief Mike Gelband. Lawrence G. McDonald, the former Lehman vice president and author of "A Colossal Failure of Common Sense," recounts Gelband's then-heretical presentation:

"He cited the shadow banks, the vast complex network of mortgage brokers that were not really banks at all but managed somehow to insert themselves into the lending process, making an enormous number of mortgages possible."

By 2017, Fannie Mae was backstopping cash-out refinancings with appraisal-free mortgages and allowing homes to be appraised using so-called "black-box appraisals"

– real estate appraisals performed by proprietary computer models. It was a return to Planet Amnesia. The reliance on this type of wizardry harkens to the computer models developed by the ratings agencies that awarded triple-A ratings to compilations of the sulfurous subprime loans.

Fannie Mae was also promoting the use of "property data collectors," a practice that keeps licensed appraisers from inspecting properties they appraise. This can't be made up.

A decade after the crisis, Fannie Mae's single-family risk management department says it no longer purchases newly originated low- or no-credit documentation, negatively amortizing, or interest-only single-family loans, nor single-family loans with prepayment penalties or balloon payments.

Allowing Fannie and Freddie, still in federal conservatorship at press time, to dictate what constitutes an appropriate appraisal would be like reuniting the U.S. fixed-income chiefs and collateral-risk bosses from Bear Stearns, Lehman Brothers, Countrywide, Ameriquest, GMAC and IndyMac and allowing them to develop future loan underwriting standards.

A decade after the crisis began, the U.S. banking industry had put the crisis firmly in its rear-view mirror. As of midyear 2017, there were 105 banks on the FDIC's problem bank list, the lowest quarter-end number since the end of the first quarter 2008, when there were 90. Earnings were at their highest level relative to average assets since the second quarter of 2007.

But in the area of consumer choice, things have never looked bleaker. Though the consolidation started years before, the number of FDIC-insured banks continued its downward spiral since the crisis. In 2007, there were more than 8,500. By 2018, that number had fallen to about 5,400. On the investment banking side, the number of public companies in the United States has also been on a steady decline, as has the number of initial public offerings. Many fault regulations and shareholder lawsuits. This trend benefits private market players at the expense of mom-and-pop investors. The regulatory state, with its additional layers of burden in the aftermath of the Subprime Crisis, has never been more oppressive and the public foots the bill.

Nota bene: The author worked as a licensed real estate appraiser during both the boom and bust phase of the great crisis. Appraisers scratched their heads in wonderment as the prices of homes were bid up during the boom phase and then withered to new lows during the bust. As long as a property is valued as of a specific date, the value will reflect market exuberance or market disfavor at the time of valuation. Just like share prices of Apple or Raytheon or Union Pacific, there is no intrinsic value for real estate. In March, investors may be willing to pay $65 a square foot for a property. By September, they may clamor to pay $75 but by the following April, they may only be willing to pay $70.

As underwriting standards eased – culminating in exotic adjustable-rate mortgages and so-called "liar loans" – more people were able to contemplate first-time home ownership, and those owning starter homes were able to contemplate a trade-up home, and up the chain it went.

Easing borrowing standards had a huge, largely uncontemplated, stimulus effect on the real estate market. An immutable law of real estate: As credit eases, the value of the collateral used to secure the credit appreciates. Conversely, as credit tightens, the value of the related collateral depreciates. It's simply supply and demand. When easy money becomes available, more participants at every level bid up a property's price.

Index

www.ingramcontent.com/pod-product-compliance
Lightning Source LLC
Chambersburg PA
CBHW071553200326
41519CB00021BB/6728